HEALING POWER

Healing Power

John Gunstone

VINE
BOOKS

Servant Books
Ann Arbor, Michigan

Cover design by Gerald L. Gawronski

Vine Books is an imprint of Servant Publications
especially designed to serve Evangelical Christians.

Published by Servant Books
P.O. Box 8617
Ann Arbor, Michigan 48107

Printed in the United States of America
ISBN 0-89283-318-1

87 88 89 90 91 10 9 8 7 6 5 4 3 2 1

Contents

Introduction

THE PRACTICE OF PRAYING for the sick with the laying on of hands (and sometimes with anointing) is growing rapidly among English-speaking Christians. While the church has always been concerned about her ministry to those who are ill, it is probably true to say that this particular form of it has not been so widespread since the early centuries. In this book I have discussed this practice and suggested what it implies for us as we seek to follow Jesus Christ in our secular society today.

I have paid special attention to the relationship between this form of ministry to the sick and spiritual renewal in local churches, principally the charismatic movement. But since the word charismatic is an important one in discussing healing as a gift of God's grace, I have reserved its use for that (its more proper theological meaning) and, to avoid confusion, referred to charismatics as "new Pentecostals."

I am grateful to many friends who have allowed me to share this ministry with them and to draw on their experiences. Among them I should mention Peter Hocken, John Richards, and Tom Stuckey, who have provided me with material from both sides of the Atlantic. Ann England has read the manuscript with the eye of a Christian doctor. Margaret, my wife, has discussed most of the things I have written in the light of her nursing career. And thanks, too, to Edward England, who suggested this topic to me. I alone am responsible for the opinions expressed here.

John Gunstone

Part One

ONE

That Other Ministry of Health

I N THE SPRING OF 1980 I spent an evening with a prayer group. It was made up of three married couples who attended an independent evangelical church. They had invited me along to lead them in a Bible study.

Before we began, one of the group, an insurance broker, handed out photocopies of a letter he had received from Norman, a friend of his. Norman had written because he was deeply concerned about a man who worked with him, Philip—or, rather, about Philip's wife, Heather. Norman wrote:

> They had been on holiday in Majorca where Heather had had a miserable time with stomach pains. On their return they went to the doctor and eventually learned that what they had put down to 'Spanish tummy' was in fact terminal cancer. Heather is not likely to live for more than a few months.
>
> She is in her mid-thirties, an extremely nice person and, like Philip, an active member of their local Roman Catholic church. They are both completely calm about their situation. Philip has said to me that if God wants Heather, it is because he knows how good she is and that she will make an excellent member of his personal congregation in heaven!

Philip has helped me a lot over the past two years, and he has asked if I will pray for his wife. This has made me feel useless and ashamed. I have not been a practicing Christian for years. Philip knows this, but he says prayer is never wasted no matter who the pray-er is. May I ask that you and possibly the members of your church would remember Philip and Heather? I only hope that, should I ever be in a similar situation to Philip's, I will be able to face things with the same calmness and strength.

The letter added that the couple had two boys, aged four and six.

In the group we discussed the letter and then prayed for Philip, Heather, and Norman before beginning our Bible study.

I had forgotten the incident until a week or two later when I found my copy of Norman's letter in a jacket pocket. As I read it again, I felt a surge of sympathy for this Roman Catholic family. I was also slightly ashamed that I hadn't prayed for them since I'd met with the group. I decided to write to them.

I don't find it easy to put together letters of this kind, least of all to people I've never met. I sat at my desk twiddling a pen and wondering what to say.

Suddenly, I was jolted to attention.

"There's no need to write. You'll meet them tomorrow."

It was as if the Lord had spoken in my ear.

I pondered those words for a long time. Next day I was to travel two hundred miles to fulfill a long-standing engagement to speak at a eucharist organized by a Roman Catholic charismatic service committee. I wondered if I would see Philip and Heather there. It seemed unlikely. They lived yet another thirty or forty miles away, and I had no indication they were interested in the charismatic renewal. Besides, Heather might not be fit to travel.

So I decided that what I had heard was the voice of my own subconscious seeking an excuse for not writing the letter. Eventually I got something down and posted it late that Friday evening. I noted that my letter had missed the last collection, so it would not be delivered until after the weekend.

The following day I arrived in time to have lunch with the committee.

"By the way," I said to the chairman as we sipped the soup, "do you happen to know Philip and Heather—?"

He put his spoon down, surprised. "No, I don't know them," he replied. "But Philip rang me up just before you arrived saying the Lord had told him to bring his wife here this afternoon. They've never been before, and he wanted to know if it would be all right for them to come. Are they friends of yours?"

I shook my head.

What a coincidence! Or was it? Was the Lord bringing us together for a special purpose?

I went over to the hall after lunch with a sense of mounting excitement.

There were three or four hundred people present. The eucharist was celebrated with much chorus singing and spontaneous prayer. When it was over, I saw a couple making their way through the crowd towards me.

"We wanted to thank you for this afternoon," they said.

"Are you Philip and Heather?" I asked.

"How did you know?"

I briefly explained how I'd heard about them. They were amazed when I said there was a letter to them in the post. They told me they'd seen the notice about the meeting in their church bulletin the previous Sunday and felt they should come. Heather looked pale, but I certainly wouldn't have recognized her as a sick woman if I'd passed her in the street.

I spoke the next words as confidently as anything I'd ever said: "Heather, I believe the Lord has arranged this meeting, so that we can anoint you and pray for your healing."

"I believe that, too," she answered firmly.

I borrowed a vial of oil from a priest. Two members of the service committee took us into a small library. Together we prayed over Philip and Heather. I anointed Heather and laid hands on her, asking the Lord to heal her.

"I'm ready to go to the Lord, if he wants me to," Heather said to me, just before I left. "I'm giving myself to him each day. But"—her voice faltered for a second—"I pray he may spare me long enough to see my little boys grow up . . ."

I traveled back home that evening feeling certain a miracle of healing was happening in her. What other explanation could there be for the astonishing way in which I met the couple? Wasn't this the kind of thing I'd often read about in books?

In the following weeks I wrote to the couple two or three times. Three months later Heather died.

Some of the evangelicals of the prayer group attended the requiem mass and funeral; they returned deeply moved by the triumphant celebration of Christ's resurrection they had shared in. In the months that followed, Philip's faith and courage in caring for his young, motherless sons was an inspiration to many. I suppose these might be regarded as a few of the blessings which arose out of Heather's death. But not for many years had my faith in Jesus Christ's commission to his church to heal the sick been so severely tested. For a long time afterwards I avoided being involved in the ministry of healing. Over and over again I wanted to say with the psalmist, "Has God forgotten to be gracious?" (Ps 77:9).

When I began my work as an Anglican priest in the 1950s, I regarded the church's ministry of healing as something which meant healing in its widest sense—the healing of relationships between God and man, between man and man, and between man and his environment. I assumed that healing in the specific sense of curing physical, mental, and emotional illnesses did not belong to the church in its local, organized form but to professionals who might or might not be Christians.

I recognized that the church can help the sick to benefit from the treatment they receive. Much illness has psychosomatic roots, so there might be a therapeutic efficacy in confession and prayer, in the assurance which the gospel brings, and in the fellowship which a local congregation offers. Indeed, in the healing of certain mental and emotional disorders, the care of a group of believers can be vital. But I was anxious that claims about the church's ministry of healing should not be pressed too far. Christians—and especially clergymen like myself—must be sensitive of the point where their role ceases and that of the doctor takes over. Diagnosis and treatment are the business of the medical profession, and that boundary must be respected.

I was extremely suspicious of those who claimed that the church might heal by spiritual means where therapy had failed. True, there were not many Christians who claimed that sort of thing back then, but I did hear about them occasionally. I argued that we must not expect God to heal us in response to our prayers any more than we should expect him to provide for us miraculously with a house on an empty lot. If we want a house, we visit a realtor and go to a bank to apply for a mortgage. Similarly, if we want to be healed, we have to go to a doctor and accept the prescribed treatment.

As a parish priest I visited the sick members of the congregation at home or in the hospital, talking with them for a while and saying the Lord's Prayer with them before I left. If they were ill for any length of time, I took them communion and added their names to the intercession list which was read out in church on Sundays. I was not aware that the prayers or the sacrament had any dynamic effect on them. Nor did I expect this. Some said they had "been helped" by the prayers and "felt better" after receiving communion, but I did not interpret this to mean any more than that they felt supported and encouraged. I certainly did not look for any remarkable gift of healing through these ministrations.

Encounter with New Pentecostals

Then, in the early 1960s I began to meet Christians who claimed that God did answer prayers for healing directly through spiritual gifts. They said that we are still living in the apostolic age of the church and that we should expect the power of the Holy Spirit to cure the afflicted just as he did in the days of Peter and Paul. They were fellow Anglicans and others who were involved in the movement for charismatic renewal which was beginning to influence the traditional denominations.

I attended meetings at which prayers were offered for the sick with a confidence I had not experienced before. People stood up and testified to miraculous cures. It was puzzling and yet exciting. Surely this was the ministry of the church to the sick as it was intended to be! I had to admit that these new Pentecostals seemed closer to the Scriptures than I was. The risen Christ said of his disciples, "They will lay their hands on the sick, and they will recover" (Mk 16:18). I glimpsed that promise being fulfilled.

But I was uneasy about some of the things I heard and read.

First of all, there was the undoubted fact that, even after much prayer, some of the sick were *not* healed. To put it crudely, the success rate among new Pentecostals in what they called "that other ministry of health" was not nearly as high as that of Jesus and his disciples. I accepted that in Jesus the living Word of God was made flesh and dwelt among us and that he was a perfect channel for God's healing grace. Nevertheless, the "failures" were evident enough to make me uneasy about the stories of miraculous healings I read about or heard recounted at meetings.

Also, their simplistic approach to the Bible jarred with my theological views. I knew, for example, that the saying of Jesus I have just quoted came from a late addition to the Gospel of Mark and that its authenticity is questioned by New Testament commentators. I also noticed that new Pentecostals tended to be selective in their use of scriptural texts: they had plenty to say about Paul's teaching on spiritual gifts in his Corinthian correspondence, but they were less forthcoming about those awkward passages in the same letter where the apostle ordered women to be silent in the Christian assembly and where he referred to baptisms undertaken for the dead!

Furthermore, the manner in which they invoked God to heal the sick disturbed me. They seemed to assume that they had an intimate knowledge of the divine will and that all they had to do was ask in order to receive. When I listened to them I had an irreverent picture of the Ancient of Days seated on his heavenly throne while basketfuls of prayer requests were brought to him by angels. He picked out those sent by new Pentecostals, nodded his head, and then waved the rest away! Would our God be as capricious as that?

Finally, they spoke and acted as if the devil really existed. They called on God to "deliver" individuals from demonic powers, and they apparently addressed evil spirits by name to order them to go to the place God had prepared for them. Some people I met said they had experienced wonderful liberations through this ministry, though stories of exorcisms that went wrong were also current. I had assumed that in contemporary Western civilization such beliefs were no longer tenable.

It was about this time that I attended a summer school held in St. Augustine's College in Canterbury, England. St. Augustine's was once a missionary training college, and on the walls of its chapel are the memorials of those who were sent out from England in the last century to work overseas and who died there. The dates reveal that some of these courageous Christians survived only a year or two before being struck down by the deadly diseases of West Africa. Where, I wondered, was the church's ministry of healing then?

But the fact that an increasing number of Anglican clergy and ministers in other denominations, joined by lay people, were prepared to launch out into direct prayer for healing impressed me. Many of them were as much aware of the problems as I was. Most of them were not simplistic in their approach to the Scriptures. They just got on with the business of praying for the sick, and saw results.

So in spite of my doubts, I started a service of prayer for healing once a month on a weekday evening in the church where I was vicar. I did not publicize it widely beyond the congregation. I suggested that those who attended should bring a prayer partner with them. The service itself was straightforward: a Bible reading, a brief address, a few prayers, silence, and then those with ailments received the laying on of hands and anointing with oil. No emotional exhortation, no singing of sentimental choruses.

The number who came was not large—never more than twenty. But over the course of several years a few were healed or helped. A woman going blind found that her sight ceased to deteriorate, and she retained her vision with the aid of glasses. A man with acute asthma was cured. A woman with a diseased spine was healed. In other cases the process of healing seemed to be accelerated. People undergoing treatment recovered more quickly than they had been led to expect.

I had one great fear. What would be the effect on a sick person if I prayed for their healing but they felt no improvement?

That fear has never completely left me. It's always lurking in the background, making my involvement in the ministry of healing something of a risk. But, for two reasons, it is no longer the hurdle it once seemed. The first is that, in praying with the sick, I have become more conscious of God's guidance than of my own doubts about how to pray for an individual. The second is that, even when there has been no obvious improvement, those who were prayed with nearly always seemed to be encouraged either to accept their illness or to prepare for death. I cannot remember anyone becoming seriously embittered because the prayer for healing was not answered as we'd hoped.

When the news of this service spread around, I was invited to address clergy gatherings and other groups about my experiences. I found this unnerving at first. To conduct a service of prayer quietly in a church is one thing; to talk about it at public meetings made up of largely sceptical audiences is another!

I once went to give a lecture at a junior clergy training conference. When I had finished my talk, which was scheduled after the evening meal, one of the attendees at the conference said, "Our in-service training officer isn't here because he slipped in the snow last week and sprained his back. Why don't you visit him and lay hands on him?"

The thought of driving that night to the town some miles away and laying hands on a reverend dignitary I'd never met daunted me. Excuses leaped to my mind, but they seemed feeble in view of what I'd been saying.

Then I had an idea.

"It'll take me about half an hour to reach him from here," I said. "If you will pray at about the time I reach his house, I'll do it."

He agreed, and thirty minutes later I was in the sick man's room. He was sitting in a robe in a chair by the bed, his face white with pain. To my relief, he looked quite pleased when I told him what his junior clergy had asked me to do.

"When you've prayed with me, I'll pray for them," he said.

We prayed together, and I laid hands on him.

"Now I'd better try to walk," he said.

I felt humbled. This man had more faith than I had!

He raised himself up, slowly stretched to his full height, and took several steps up and down the room.

"I haven't been able to do that for a week," he commented. "It certainly seems much easier."

Experiences such as these gradually nudged me towards new Pentecostals and others in the church who teach that, in addition to the cures which come through the skill and care of the medical and nursing professions, healing can come directly from God in answer to prayer. I found myself in a varied company, from Roman Catholic monks and nuns who had been formed into teaching teams to introduce the ministry of healing to parishes, to pastors and elders of congregations whose theology was a long way from the high Anglicanism in which I had been reared. Yet it was a company united in the hope that God still does reach out his hand to intervene in our affairs and that his commission through Christ to heal the sick is as valid today as it was when it was given. In other words, they expected miraculous healings.

Miraculous Healing

There is a stumbling block in our approach to the ministry of healing. We are children of our scientific age. We assume that, with the development of modern medicine, it is now possible to find a cure for all our pains and ills. If an unknown disease appears, like the acquired immunity defence syndrome, we tell ourselves that one day research will discover the appropriate vaccine or treatment for it. We don't think of any other kind of cure.

Medical science seems to leave no place for a miracle in the New Testament sense. Most illnesses can be diagnosed and treated according to certain well-tried principles. Various afflictions have a natural history which can be read about in medical textbooks. For example, a straightforward fracture will be healed over a number of weeks, provided the ends of the broken bone are placed together and kept in close alignment. Different fractures take different lengths of time, but the course and history of each type is known. If the healing of the fracture is delayed, this is either because some mechanical factor required for healing is absent (the ends of the bone may not be properly aligned), or because the health and vitality of the person with the fracture is impaired. Stories of fractures that were healed through prayer are not included!

Some illnesses have a natural history which includes remissions: these are phases in which the disease process is arrested and in which there may be indications of an improvement before a further relapse takes place. Usually these remissions and relapses are difficult to predict. Very occasionally an illness will be healed without any obvious reason. Certain kinds of cancer may show spontaneous healing. Most doctors have at least one tale of a patient who suddenly recovered in spite of the gloomiest prognosis. We cannot with integrity call such healings miraculous, for it could well be that one day the causes of these phenomena will be discovered.

In fact, trying to prove medically that a miracle has happened in the course of a healing is fraught with problems.

1. There is much uncertainty about what actually constitutes a miracle. The more scientific medicine discovers about the human body's resources for repair after injury, the more wonderful the human body turns out to be. The combination of mechanisms and

chemical changes involved in effecting a repair is baffling in its complexity. I once heard a professor of hematology describe with awe what he observed when blood cells went into action to heal a wound. He was not less ecstatic than a speaker at a conference describing how he had been healed in answer to prayer.

2. Many healings are more functional than organic. An individual has a pain. The doctor can find nothing but prescribes a mild drug. The individual then goes to church and receives prayer with the laying on of hands for healing. The pain disappears. For the individual, that was a miraculous healing—and, in a way, he has a right to call it that, for the pain which he suffered has amazingly been taken away. Nobody doubts the reality of psychosomatic causes of illnesses. But the evidence is not sufficient for his doctor to call it a miracle.

3. Assembling evidence to prove that a healing was miraculous is a complex business. In terms of scientific medicine, it has to be demonstrated that an organic disease has completely disappeared, either through direct observation, or through an X-ray, or through an examination of a piece of the tissue. An ideal example would be where a severe case had been examined and tested by two specialists in that disease. The sick person would not be given any therapy but would be allowed to attend a service of prayer for healing. Afterwards, that sick person would then be examined and tested again by those two specialists, and then undergo a further examination some months later. If, after all that, it could be shown that the disease had completely disappeared between the first and the second examinations, it could be claimed tentatively that a miracle had happened. No wonder so few such healings are certified medically at Lourdes and elsewhere!

In this scientific atmosphere, it is not surprising that a good deal of contemporary theology all but rules out the possibility of miraculous healings. Living in such a highly technological culture, biblical commentators and other theologians have tried to explain the miraculous element in the Gospels in a scientific manner. They suggest that Jesus didn't really multiply the loaves and the fishes, or walk on the water, or still the storm: these stories arose out of Christ's involvement with human need and danger, and this is how the evangelists recorded the memory of his involvements. They imply that there was no physical resurrection of Christ's corpse on the first

Easter morning: this belief arose out of the apostles' awareness of the Lord's continuing presence after his crucifixion. Many scholars similarly put forward medical and psychological theories for the healings and exorcisms done by Jesus and his disciples.

I was, as I have said, brought up in this kind of theological teaching. Yet as I became more involved in the church's ministry of healing, I met Christians, including some doctors, who encouraged me to be open to the possibility of a miraculous response to prayer. Aware of the great mystery behind the healing process, the leap of faith required to hope for a miracle did not seem so daunting for them. They could have said to me, as Hamlet said to his companion, "There are more things in heaven and earth, Horatio, than are dreamt of in your philosophy."

So questions about how to relate seemingly miraculous healings to scientific medicine no longer appeared so important. Occasionally I witnessed remarkable healings in response to prayer, and I am thankful to describe them as miraculous, especially when they direct those involved to the Lord.

Which leads me to a definition of a miraculous healing which I offer for those who still find the questions troublesome:

It is an extraordinary cure which is both perceived with the eye of faith and which also builds up faith.

Let me unpack that definition to spell out what it implies.

An extraordinary cure. It's out of the ordinary, beyond the present limits of medical knowledge and experience, including healings which come through psychotherapy. True, a miracle in one generation may seem ordinary in the next as a result of scientific research; but that does not rob the extraordinary cure of its extraordinariness to those who observe it. Nor does it mean that all miraculous healings will one day seem to be very ordinary!

Which is both perceived with the eye of faith. If an extraordinary cure is not perceived with the eye of faith—or at least, with the eye that is willing to seek in faith—then it becomes just a coincidence or "something we don't understand yet." Tell a story of a miraculous healing and watch the different reactions of those who listen. Some will say, "What a miracle! Praise the Lord!" But others will retort, "That's remarkable, but there must be an explanation somewhere!" I don't want to be judgmental about the second group of listeners. I just want to emphasize that the extraordinary healing only becomes miraculous in the New Testament sense of the word when our faith is engaged by it.

...And which also builds up faith. But it is not enough just to believe that a miracle has taken place. Any gullible soul might do that. Our faith should also be built up by it. A miraculous healing is a wonderful gift, and we can rejoice with those who receive it; but the purpose of such a healing does not end with the relief from pain or the recovery from a disability. The healings of Christ pointed to the kingdom of God. If, as a result of such a healing, we are not led to praise God, then there is a sense in which the extraordinary cure was not a true miracle, for the healing was not complete. We shall explore the significance of this further on in the book.

The question is sometimes raised that if Christ healed the sick and raised the dead, why don't we expect him to work resurrections nowadays if we hope that he will heal miraculously?

I must confess, I cannot think of anything remotely adequate to write about this. Some years ago I met an Indian pastor who assured me with earnest sincerity that he had seen three dead people brought back to life in answer to prayer, and I've no doubt that for him they were astonishing miracles (extraordinary events which were both perceived with the eye of faith and which also built up faith). But obviously any attempt to establish the medical proof of such events (coupled with the problem of identifying the moment of death in the human body) is impossible. Indeed, like all miraculous experiences, there is something strangely elusive when we try to establish the scientific proof of extraordinary events following prayer. In the end, we are thrown back on our faith in what God can do, not on the assurance which we are tempted to seek in human ingenuity.

All I can say is that I believe that God can raise the dead back to this life and that there may be occasions when he does so. If those occasions are extremely rare, that may be because we lack the faith either to hope or to perceive them. Or it may be that he wills they should be extremely rare. Such resurrections, after all, were not a prominent feature of Jesus' own ministry. One was the outcome of a request for healing (Jairus's daughter, Mk 5:21-43), another was a spontaneous act of compassion (the widow's son at Nain, Lk 7:11-17), and the third was a response to bereaved friends (Lazarus, Jn 11:1-44).

The miraculous, then, is one aspect of the church's ministry of healing, but it is by no means the whole of it. We are in danger of limiting that ministry if we cease to hope for extraordinary cures, but we limit it also in another way if we only look for the miraculous and not for the healings which come from God in so many different forms. The healing I am mainly concerned with in this book is "that other ministry of health" which centers on prayer and which can include the laying on of hands and anointing. Yet I intend to demonstrate that this ministry of healing is intimately linked with all that is done for the relief of the sick, not only through the Christian community but also through the goodness of women and men everywhere who are moved with compassion for those with pains, distresses, and disabilities.

Because the church's ministry of healing centers on prayer, it depends on movements of spiritual renewal which encourage Christians to greater faith and more persistent intercession. In our generation the new Pentecostal movement is doing much in nearly all denominations across the world to encourage greater faith; it is largely responsible for the restoration of the ministry of healing which we are witnessing in the churches today. We must, then, examine this movement carefully. But the Holy Spirit is not confined just to certain groups within the Christian community. Other spiritual renewals have influenced this restoration, so we must consider them, too.

This, then, is our theme: the interaction of renewal in the Holy Spirit with the church's ministry of healing.

But where should we begin? With the healing miracles of Jesus, to show how that wonderful ministry has been continued in the church since the days of the apostles in the power of the Spirit? That, after all, is where the majority of books about the ministry of healing begin.

I don't think so. Just to look at the healing miracles of Jesus without putting them into the context of his life, death, resurrection, and ascension, seems to me to distort the truth. The story of his passion and crucifixion reminds us that he who healed the sick and raised the dead also prayed that he might be spared his destined pain and execution. And we remember also that, as he hung on the cross, the bystanders sneered, "He saved others; let him save himself, if he is the Christ of God, his Chosen One" (Lk 23:35).

Jesus was, and is, our wounded healer. The cross was the cost he paid for our healing, and the cross remains the source of the church's ministry of healing—as, indeed, it is the source of our spiritual renewal. We live if we also die with him. Only when I see the healings of Christ through the light of his sacrifice do I dare to hope that the tragedies I encounter in the ministry of healing might, in God's mercy, be glorious triumphs after all.

That is where I want to begin.

TWO

The Wounds of
Our Healer

T HE REVELATION THAT GOD WOULD HEAL his people through
the wounds of his Servant gradually unfolded through the
experience of Israel, whose writers recorded that experience in the
books of the Old Testament. Closely allied to this revelation was
Israel's reaction to human suffering, especially her own suffering as
God's people. It will, I think, be useful if we look at some of the
reasons for suffering we find in the Old Testament, for they will help
us to approach the mystery of Christ's passion and death, and so also
his ministry of healing. This approach does not solve the dark
problem of pain; but the revelation of the mystery encourages us to
hope that what we and others suffer in this life is not beyond the
ultimate purposes of God, even if at times bitter personal experience
makes that revelation difficult to accept.

What biblical scholars call the theodicy of the Old Testament—
that is, the way it vindicates the righteousness of God in spite of the
existence of evil in the world—is a complicated study. Different
layers of teaching have come from the centuries before Christ, and
these teachings have intermixed as the books of the Old Testament
took shape. I will list five of the reasons for human suffering which
the Old Testament offers us, and I will note how the apostolic
writers, for whom the Old Testament was the word of God,

17

interpreted the cross in the light of its wisdom. I will also indicate how some of these Old Testament concepts have persisted in the church's attitudes towards suffering.

1. *Sickness and suffering are signs of the spiritual warfare which God wages against evil powers.*

Dualism (the belief that pains and misfortunes are caused by demonic forces) is one of the most ancient solutions to the problem of suffering. We find this concept behind the earliest traditions in the Old Testament. In Genesis, God won the preliminary battle against the principalities and powers when he brought the watery chaos under his control, and one of the lessons of the story of Adam and Eve is that the cosmic battle would continue until God had finally defeated all his enemies. The dualistic concept unfolds in the Old Testament to show that God's foes are devious and cunning and that they strike his people with sickness and suffering in unexpected ways and at critical moments.

This dualism was not absolute, however, for later traditions acknowledged that if God really is Lord of all creation, then even evil powers must in some way be subject to him. It was, after all, God himself who condemned Adam and Eve to a life of suffering after the fall, and he could hardly have done that if the suffering had not been within his permissive will. The Book of Job, which struggled with the problem of suffering more than any other Old Testament work, begins with a scene from the heavenly court in which Satan seeks and is given permission by God to test the Lord's faithful servant, Job, by inflicting on him a loathsome disease and bringing disaster on his family. Then, in a lengthy poem, it explores the various reasons for human suffering offered by the religion of Israel and finds them inadequate.

Among the healings recorded in the Old Testament is one that is a kind of exorcism. When Saul was pestered by an evil spirit (sent by God), he was delivered from it when David played on his lyre (1 Sm 16:14ff). But the question remained: how can a good God have dealings with what is evil? Gradually there arose in the later Old Testament era a conviction that the problem would be solved supernaturally. A new age would dawn when God would usher in his kingdom, and the devil and his evil minions would forever be overthrown in a cataclysmic clash between the forces of light and the forces of darkness. God's intervention in human history would result in the divine victory over Satan and his hordes. This conviction came to the fore in Jewish writings in the two centuries immediately before Christ in what is known as apocalyptic (revelatory) literature, which formed the background to certain New Testament ideas. For example, Enoch 1:9 says that evil will be banished when the Lord comes with thousands of his holy ones to execute judgment upon all and destroy the ungodly.

About one fifth of Christ's healings involved rebuking evil spirits. Jesus came, he said, to overpower the strong man, the devil (Lk 11:21-22). The spiritual warfare between Christ and Satan began after Christ's baptism in the river Jordan, continued throughout his ministry, and culminated in his suffering and death on the cross. Calvary appeared to be a victory of evil over good; but God reversed the victory by raising his Son from the grave. Paul taught the significance of this by describing it in terms of a military parade: "He disarmed the principalities and powers and made a public example of them, triumphing over them in him." (Col 2:15). The picture is one of a conquering hero leading his army back to his capital city with his enemies as prisoners in his triumphant procession.

Jesus' ministry to those troubled by evil spirits, then, foreshadowed what he was to accomplish on the cross. The deliverance of Satan's victims is a sign that the kingdom of God is breaking into the experience of the women and men of New Testament times. "The light shines in the darkness, but the darkness has not overcome it" (Jn 1:5).

Some New Testament scholars argue that the illnesses Christ healed through exorcisms would nowadays be tackled medically. They suggest that the man whom Jesus saw lurking among the tombs was suffering from an acute form of hysteria which threw him into uncontrollable paroxysms, breaking his fetters and terrifying a herd of swine (Mk 5:1-10), and that the child who was deaf and dumb was the victim of epileptic fits, causing accidents which were ascribed to demons (Mk 9:14-29). But other commentators feel these suggestions do less than justice to the New Testament writers, who carefully distinguished exorcisms from other forms of healing in Jesus' ministry, or to the experience of the church throughout the ages, including the present day.

Scientific man may want to reject dualism and assert that belief in the devil is a superstition which belongs to the past; but it is not so easy to ignore what continues to happen in the battle against disease. Modern medicine makes no more allowance for demonic influence than for miraculous healing as an explanation of physical phenomena; but that does not constitute conclusive proof that demons do not exist. There are countless people today whose healing has been given through deliverance ministries in which the evil in them has been named and expelled with the authority of Jesus' name. Dennis Nineham, one of the most "demythologizing" of New Testament scholars, was wise when he concluded his notes on the narrative of the Gerasene demoniac in Mark 5 with a quotation from another writer: "It is not profitable to attempt rationalizing versions of what may have occurred."

2. Sickness and sufferings are means by which God punishes us for our sins.

According to this penal concept, the first man and the first woman brought disobedience to the human race; as a consequence, God condemned Adam to the toil of laboring for the support of his family while Eve was inflicted with the pain of childbirth and ultimately with death (Gn 3:16-24). Their descendants—the entire human race—still suffer for sin through sickness and disease as well as through natural calamities and the violence of enemies.

The Book of Deuteronomy interpreted the story of Israel in this light. Its editors saw that story as a fourfold cycle: the people are unfaithful; God chastises them with suffering; they turn to him with cries for mercy and help; he restores them once more as the people of his covenant (Dt 4:25-32). Similarly, the individual can expect to be punished when he sins: "O Lord, be gracious to me; heal me, for I have sinned against thee!" (Ps 41:4). Conversely, healing is a sign that transgressions have been forgiven: "O Lord my God, I cried to thee for help, and thou hast healed me" (Ps 30:2).

These and similar passages present us with an image of God as a wrathful deity who avenges disobedience to his will with pain and death. The image appears over and over again in the Old Testament. One of the classic pictures of it is in the words of Job's visitors, who urge the sufferer to repent of his sins rather than blame God for what has happened to him: "He strikes them for their wickedness / in the sight of men, / because they turned aside from following him, / and had no regard for any of his ways" (Jb 34:26-27).

But even when this poem was being edited, the protest was already being raised against such a crude notion of God's vindictiveness. Would a just God punish the innocent? Job had been obedient to the divine law; he had done nothing to deserve such suffering at the hands of the Almighty: "If I have walked with falsehood, / and my foot has hastened to deceit; / (Let me be weighed in a just balance, / and let God know my integrity!) (Jb 31:5-6).

The apostolic church saw in the cross Christ's willing acceptance of the consequences of sin on man's behalf. The Son, the sinless and innocent one, suffered the punishment due to sin in place of disobedient women and men. Deserving only the wrath of God, we have been rescued by what Jesus has done. "Since, therefore, we are now justified by his blood, much more shall we be saved by him from the wrath of God" (Rom 5:9). Paul's words come near to suggesting that Jesus suffered what sinful man should have suffered in order to propitiate an angry deity. But the apostle did not go quite as far as that. The Father was not venting his anger on the Son. Rather, the Son participated so fully in the human condition that he entered into the effects of sin—into the suffering and death which are the lot of every woman and man—without himself being tainted with sin.

It is, of course, a mistake to interpret the wrath of God in terms of human anger. The ancient view of God as one who became angry with his people was refined as it was recognized that the divine wrath is the opposite of divine love. Because he is holy and just, God cannot love sin and evil, and therefore his permanent attitude towards them is designated as his wrath. It is a quality of God's nature without which he would cease to be righteous and his love would degenerate into sentimentality.

Yet the belief that God punishes the sinner with sickness in various forms persists. I was talking to a couple of nuns one day when the name of a Roman Catholic priest was mentioned. Some years previously this man had left the ordained ministry in order to marry. Since the nuns had known him, I thought they would be interested to hear I had met him and his wife.

"They have two children," I added, "But sadly one of them is hydrocephalic."

I had expected them to be sympathetic, but that was not their immediate reaction.

"It was the Lord's punishment on him," one of them said gravely.

The other nodded.

I was so shocked it took me a few seconds to grasp what they meant. These were two kindly Christian women, yet they apparently regarded the child's disability as a form of divine vengeance because of the actions of its father, who had not been allowed to resign as a priest because applications for laicizations were being refused by the Vatican at the time.

3. *Sickness and suffering are means through which God educates his people and leads them to greater obedience.*

The prophets interpreted the defeats and disasters which Israel endured in this way: "I have heard Ephraim bemoaning, / 'Thou hast chastened me, and I was chastened, / like an untrained calf; / bring me back that I may be restored, / for thou art the Lord my God. / For after I had turned away I repented; / and after I was instructed, / I smote upon my thigh; / I was ashamed, and I was confounded, / because I bore the disgrace of my youth'" (Jer 31:18-19).

The Wisdom writers said that suffering could be interpreted as a sign that God cares for us. Sickness is like a spanking from a parent who loves his child and wants him to distinguish right from wrong (in an age which had no doubts about the benefits of corporal punishment!). "The Lord reproves him whom he loves, / as a father the son in whom he delights" (Prv 3:12). Job's friends took the same view, telling him that his sufferings were a blessing in disguise: "Behold, happy is the man whom God reproves; / therefore despise not the chastening of the Almighty. / For he wounds, but he binds up; / he smites, but his hands heal" (Jb 5:17-18).

This concept of parental discipline was applied to the cross, and the author of the Letter to the Hebrews taught that the passion of Christ was intended by the Father as a means of testing the Son's fidelity as the latter shared the life of fallen humanity:

"Although he was a Son, he learned obedience through what he suffered; and being made perfect he became the source of eternal salvation to all who obey him" (Heb 5:8-9). The author did not say that the Son learned to obey through his sufferings as one who did not know what obedience was. Rather, the Son learned obedience in the only way possible in an incarnate life—through submission to the will of the Father in a series of situations leading to the supreme test of all. It was an obedience made perfect in suffering in the sense of being refined and demonstrated. Christ's obedience to God first emerged when as a boy his parents found him in the temple ("Did you not know that I must be in my Father's house?" [Lk 2:49]) and reached its climax in Gethsemane ("Father, if thou art willing, remove this cup from me; nevertheless not my will, but thine, be done" [Lk 22:42]). He took his obedience to the utmost point: "Unto death, even death on a cross" (Phil 2:8).

Sickness as a means of correction and as a test of faithfulness to God passed into Christian teaching and influenced strongly the church's ministry to the sick. Medieval prayers for the invalid included a petition to "give your servant grace so to take your correction, that after this painful life is ended, he may dwell in life everlasting." One of the most famous—or infamous—expositions of this view is in the order for the visitation of the sick in the *Book of Common Prayer* (1662) where the minister is enjoined to exhort the invalid:

> Dearly beloved, know this, that Almighty God is the Lord of life and death, and of all things to them pertaining, as youth, strength, health, age, weakness, and sickness. Wherefore, whatsoever your sickness is, know you certainly, that it is God's visitation. And for what cause soever this sickness is sent unto you; whether it be to try your patience, for the example of others, and that your faith may be found in the day of the Lord laudable, glorious, and honorable, to the increase of glory and endless felicity; or else it be sent unto you to correct and amend in you whatsoever doth offend the eyes of your heavenly Father; know you certainly, that if you truly repent you of your sins, and bear your sickness patiently, trusting in God's mercy for his dear Son Jesus Christ's sake, and render unto him humble thanks for his fatherly visitation, submitting yourself wholly unto his will, it shall turn to your profit, and help you forward in the right way that leadeth unto everlasting life.

We would not want to say nowadays that God sends suffering in order to teach us a lesson. Our vision of God is not one of a stern, supernatural schoolmaster. Yet certain inflictions at particular moments in our lives can have an educative result—if only to help us appreciate better what others have to endure. Where personal pain leads to deeper compassion, or where it enlightens us in other ways to the wisdom of God's law, then it becomes a means of discipleship.

This is what the author of Hebrews went on to explain after describing how Jesus learned obedience through his sufferings: quoting the same verses from Proverbs, he wrote, "For they disciplined us for a short time at their pleasure, but he disciplines us for our good, that we may share his holiness. For the moment all discipline seems painful rather than pleasant; later it yields the peaceful fruit of righteousness to those who have been trained by it" (Heb 12:10-11). He was, it is true, referring specifically to the hardships which faced his brethren as Christians in a hostile, pagan society, but sickness and disability were also in his mind, for he continued, "Therefore lift your drooping hands and strengthen your weak knees, and make straight paths for your feet, so that what is lame may not be put out of joint but rather be healed" (Heb 12:12-13).

If sickness has an educative result, that is something the patient has to discover for himself; it is not something on which he can be admonished as the *Book of Common Prayer* tried to do.

4. *Suffering and sickness in this life are insignificant when compared with the blessings God has for his people in the future.*

We have already noted that the hope of a new age in which God would be vindicated and other nations would recognize in Israel a privileged path to God was a feature of later Jewish apocalyptic writing. Then the righteous would be rewarded and the wicked would receive what they deserve. The parable of the rich man and Lazarus in the New Testament reflects this expectation when the roles of the two characters are reversed after death: the rich man suffers in Hades while the poor man sits beside Abraham in the feast of heaven (Lk 16:19-31). In the religion of Israel this was the kind of future towards which all history was converging and, when that time arrived, what was suffered in this life would be seen to be of no account compared with the bliss that followed. Closely associated with this hope of a future blessedness was belief in the coming of the Lord's Anointed, as we shall see in the next section.

Belief in a life after death only emerged slowly in the Old Testament, but in Christian teaching Jewish apocalyptic hopes were transformed into a belief in the second coming of Christ, the judgment of God, and resurrection to eternal life in the kingdom of heaven. The resurrection and ascension of Jesus caught up that hope and showed that it sprang from the one, unique moment when the Son of God suffered and died on the cross. So Christians, too, in the midst of their sufferings can look forward in faith to future blessings: "I consider that the sufferings of this present time are not worth comparing with the glory that is to be revealed to us" (Rom 8:18); "Blessed be the God and Father of our Lord Jesus Christ! By his great mercy we have been born anew to a living hope through the resurrection of Jesus Christ from the dead. . . . In this you rejoice, though now for a little while you may have to suffer various trials" (1 Pt 1:3, 6).

One of the reasons why the church has often failed to pray for the healing of the sick is that we have tended to interpret the apocalyptic hope of the Old and New Testaments in terms of what we can look forward to in heaven. Sufferers were consequently encouraged to accept their afflictions with fortitude rather than with petitions for healing. A familiar attitude (reflected in the quotation from the *Book of Common Prayer*) was that if you accepted your cross nobly in this life, you would be rewarded with a glorious crown beyond the grave.

Francis MacNutt, in his book *Healing* (1974), criticized this attitude among his fellow Roman Catholics. The result of it was, he said, that in their minds suffering and sanctity had been wedded together in a widely held opinion that the endurance of pain was a necessary qualification for spiritual maturity. He also pointed out that the cross which Jesus invited his disciples to carry represented the sufferings inflicted on them by others, largely through persecution, and that this invitation did not mean they should not seek for healing when they were ill.

Nevertheless, when we pray for healing, for others as well as for ourselves, we know that one day we and they will not be cured. We shall all die. Our prayers apparently will not have been answered and the world will say that our ministry has "failed." But such a conclusion is to ignore what the gospel is ultimately about. Although

Jesus had great compassion on the sick and healed them, we sense that his eyes were always looking beyond this life, to a kingdom which flashed in and through his earthly ministry but which was to be found in its fullness beyond this existence. "In my Father's house are many rooms; if it were not so, would I have told you that I go there to prepare a place for you?" (Jn 14:2).

Death is the gateway to our final healing. That is why we pray, in the words of an ancient and beautiful text used at requiems and funeral services: "May God in his infinite love and mercy bring us and the whole church, living and departed in the Lord Jesus Christ, to a joyful resurrection and the fulfilment of his eternal kingdom."

5. *Sickness and suffering are the consequences of being God's obedient servant in this world.*

This is not a prominent concept in the Old Testament as a whole, but it is expressed vividly in the songs of the suffering servant in Isaiah (42:1-4; 49:1-7; 50:4-11; 52:13-15; 53:1-12). Whether this servant was an historical person or whether he represented corporately Israel itself or some group in it, we learn from the songs that he was conscious of his vocation as God's servant and that in a mysterious way that vocation involved him in suffering.

He was chosen and upheld by God's Spirit for his task. The Lord says: "Behold my servant, whom I uphold, my chosen, in whom my soul delights; / I have put my Spirit upon him, / he will bring forth justice to the nations" (Is 42:1). The servant was told by God to gather together the scattered people of Israel and to reveal to them the divine will. He was brutally treated by those to whom he preached God's word, yet in the midst of that agonizing experience he knew the Lord's power strengthening him: "For the Lord God helps me; / therefore I have not been confounded . . . / He who vindicates me is near" (Is 50:7-8).

For their part, the people rejected him because there was nothing about him that drew them to him. He said nothing in self-defence or in explanation of his vocation: "He had no form or comeliness that we should look at him, / and no beauty that we should desire him. / He was despised and rejected by men; / a man of sorrows, and acquainted with grief. . . . / He was oppressed, and he was afflicted, / yet he opened not his mouth; / like a lamb that is led to the slaughter, / and like a sheep that before its shearers is dumb, so he opened not his mouth" (Is 53:2, 7).

Eventually, the true nature of the servant's mission was recognized. His was a vicarious suffering, for he substituted himself for those who would otherwise have had to suffer instead: "Surely he has borne our griefs / and carried our sorrows; / yet we esteemed him stricken, smitten by God, and afflicted. / But he was wounded for our transgressions, he was bruised for our iniquities; / upon him was the chastisement that made us whole, / and with his stripes we are healed" (Is 53:4-5). Mysteriously the servant's suffering was not what it seemed—the unjust infliction of pain on an innocent man. It was a sacrificial offering through which God established a covenant with his people: "Yet it was the will of the Lord to bruise him; / he has put him to grief; / when he makes himself an offering for sin, / he shall see his offspring, he shall prolong his days; / the will of the Lord shall prosper in his hand; / he shall see the fruit of the travail of his soul and be satisfied; / by his knowledge shall the righteous one, my servant, / make many to be accounted righteous; / and he shall bear their iniquities" (Is 53:10-11).

Close in thought to the songs of the suffering servant of God are the closing chapters of the Book of Job. After his visitors had failed to satisfy him with their traditional explanations for his plight, Job in the end appealed to God directly, and God spoke. He did not take up Job's question about his unjust treatment and the problem of innocent suffering, but by giving Job a vision of his divine wisdom and power, Job was brought to the point where he could acknowledge that God is great and wise. Job then repented of his angry words and admitted that his own vindication was of no consequence once he had experienced communion with God: "Therefore I have uttered what I did not understand, / things too wonderful for me, which I did not know. / ... I had heard of thee by the hearing of the ear, / but now my eye sees thee; / therefore I despise myself, / and repent in dust and ashes" (Jb 42:3-6).

The Book of Job does not answer the problem of suffering—particularly the suffering that overwhelms the faithful servant of God—but it does affirm that God uses suffering for his purposes and that he is not detached and distant from what his servant endures.

Such passages from Isaiah and Job prepare for a revelation of God's love through the cross and for a discipleship that includes suffering as well as healing. Only once did Jesus explicitly attribute to himself the songs of the suffering servant: "For I tell you that this scripture must be fulfilled in me, 'And he was reckoned with transgressors'; for what is written about me has its fulfilment" (Lk 22:37, quoting Is 53:12). But the reference is implicit in the narrative of the last supper: "This is my blood of the covenant, which is poured out for many" (Mk 14:24, the words "for many" echoing Is 42:6 and 49:8). And Job's cry "For I know that my Redeemer lives, / and at last he will stand upon the earth" (19:25) became the prophetic promise of the resurrection for the church.

The narratives of the passion, it is believed, go back to the earliest accounts of Christ's ministry. These stories were circulated orally in the apostolic church before they were written down and included in the Gospels; and, as they were told, Old Testament passages sprang to new and precious significance as preachers and writers realized how the events witnessed by the apostles fulfilled what God had said to Israel of old. According to an early tradition, it was the risen Christ himself who pointed the apostles to the Old Testament for a revelation of what he had done: "And beginning with Moses and all the prophets, he interpreted to them in all the scriptures the things concerning himself" (Lk 24:27). In the Old Testament the Spirit of God had been at work, preparing for Christ's death and resurrection: "The prophets who prophesied of the grace that was to be yours . . . they inquired what person or time was indicated by the Spirit of Christ within them predicting the sufferings of Christ and the subsequent glory" (1 Pt 1:10-11).

So the Scriptures confirmed the apostle's belief that Christ's death had not been fortuitous; it had been willed and determined by God, and it formed part of the winding up of his eternal purpose, standing on the frontier between the present age and the age to come. Thus Paul could write, "Christ died for our sins in accordance with the scriptures" (1 Cor 15:3), and the fourth evangelist could describe the course of Christ's suffering and death in terms that showed God's purpose was moving towards its completion because "this was to fulfil the scripture" (Jn 19:24). The Old Testament had prophesied that God would heal his people through the wounds of his servant. Suffering and healing come together when God's saving grace in Jesus Christ is revealed.

Salvation and Healing

We tend to relate salvation only to our spiritual state. We select texts which refer to the day of judgment (e.g., "salvation is nearer to us now than when we first believed" [Rom 13:11]), forgetting that in the Bible, salvation has a fuller meaning. In its Old Testament roots it means "to be wide," "to create space," "to develop without hindrance," and thence "to have victory in battle" (1 Sam 14:6-14). Any leader who gained a victory over the people's foes (and so gave them space to live without hindrance) was said to be their "savior" (Jgs 2:18). But since it was God who raised up these leaders, then the people's real savior was none other than God himself. Israel looked back on her own history as the story of how God became her savior through divinely appointed agents.

Under the new covenant that divinely appointed agent was revealed in Jesus Christ—the "Author of . . . salvation" whom God made "perfect through suffering" (Heb 2:10). He is *the* agent of God whom other agents of God had prefigured. His name, Jesus, or Joshua, means "God saves." The first Joshua led the people into the promised land through a successful military campaign; the second Joshua won salvation for his people in a spiritual battle that involved his suffering, death, and resurrection. And his healings were prophetic signs that salvation was at hand: "Then the eyes of the blind shall be opened, / and the ears of the deaf unstopped; / then shall the lame man leap like a hart, / and the tongue of the dumb sing for joy (Is 35:5-6). Jesus sometimes used the verb "to save" when he healed (e.g., "Daughter, your faith has saved you" [Mk 5:34 margin]). But he never used it to refer to a single organ or limb of the body—always to refer to the whole person. From this we learn that salvation goes beyond physical healing although it sometimes includes it.

Healing is that which leads to health; and health is the state in which we experience complete and successful functioning of every part of our being in harmonious relationship with God and with one another and our environment. In our language "health," "whole," "holy," and "hale" are all derived from the old English word "hal," which means "complete." Healing, then, is what God gives his people to fulfil his purposes for them in body, mind, and spirit, and the church's ministry of healing is a demonstration of the salvation which God offers through Jesus Christ in the power of the Holy Spirit. That is why a healing which does not result in bringing the one who is healed to an acknowledgment that Jesus Christ is Savior and Lord is less than what a Christian understands by complete healing—salvation. Repentance and faith are very much part of the healing process.

But salvation will not be fulfilled until the second coming of Christ. The victory he has won can only be foretasted now as we are being led out of sin into the new life of his Spirit. One of the signs of that victory can be physical healing, but such a sign is not guaranteed for the disciples of the Crucified. Although the power of sin and death has been broken through the cross, the effect that they have on humanity remains until the last day.

From time to time in the history of the church, groups have claimed that because Christians are being saved by God, they should experience that salvation in perfect health. They should never be ill; and when illness does inflict them, they should shake it off swiftly through the healing power of their Savior.

In some respects, this teaching is a reaction against those Old Testament views of suffering which, as we have seen, have persisted in the church and lowered Christians' expectation of what God might do miraculously for the sick. It reaffirms that disease is an intrusion into God's good creation and that disease is the result of the devil's malicious activity.

But it goes too far. Since the Son of God won salvation through suffering and death, we cannot expect to escape suffering any more than we shall escape death itself. We should be able to affirm joyfully with Paul that "the life of Jesus may also be manifested in our bodies" (2 Cor 4:10) and that the power of Jesus "is made perfect in weakness" (2 Cor 12:9). But it will not be until the general resurrection that "death shall be no more, neither shall there be mourning nor crying nor pain" (Rev. 21:4).

To assert that healing is as readily and instantly available as salvation, or that a believer has no business to be ill, is to try to anticipate the resurrection and the redemption of our bodies beyond what the New Testament teaches. The lifting up of the Son of Man on the cross was the healing moment for mankind, prefigured in the lifting up of the bronze serpent in the wilderness for the healing of the Israelites (Nm 21:4-9). The disciples of Christ cannot expect less.

So in the early church the experiences of suffering and healing were woven together in a strange paradox. Both Peter and Paul healed the sick, but both of them eventually came to a martyr's death in Rome. What happened to them mattered little. Their priority was to serve Jesus Christ as their Lord and to proclaim the gospel of the kingdom. Imprisonments and the trials were just as much occasions for manifestations of the Holy Spirit as miraculous healings were. In everything they relied on the power of God. "Yes, and I shall rejoice," wrote Paul from prison, "for I know that through your prayers and the help of the Spirit of Jesus Christ this will turn out for my salvation" (Phil 1:19 margin).

Indeed, this spirit of triumphant expectancy led the apostolic church to interpret its sufferings as a means of union with Jesus Christ in his passion. Paul could boast about his sufferings on behalf of the gospel because they demonstrated God's power in the midst of his weakness (2 Cor 11:16). When an affliction remained with him in spite of prayer for healing, he accepted it as a means through which God told him, "My grace is sufficient for you, for my power is made perfect in weakness" (2 Cor 12:9).

Christian slaves, who were liable to ill treatment at the hands of unscrupulous masters, were urged to accept their fate as a way of following Christ: "For to this you have been called, because Christ also suffered for you, leaving you an example" (1 Pt 2:21). To endure persecution faithfully was to be joined to Christ, to be washed with the blood of the Lamb, and to be in the front ranks of the worshipping multitudes in heaven (Rv 7:14).

We find this acceptance of suffering as a mystical sharing in the passion of Christ in different parts of the New Testament. Luke portrayed the death of Stephen in such a way that the details of his execution—the prayer for the forgiveness of his persecutors, his handing over of his spirit to God—is like a rerun of the crucifixion of Jesus (Acts 7:59-60). In Philippians 3:10-11 Paul expressed his deep yearning for union with Christ in his passion and death: "that I may know him and the power of his resurrection, and may share his sufferings, becoming like him in his death, that if possible I may attain the resurrection from the dead." In another passage he dared to suggest that the pain which a faithful Christian endures within the fellowship of the Spirit is a fulfilling of what Christ endured on the cross: "Now I rejoice in my sufferings for your sake, and in my flesh I complete what is lacking in Christ's afflictions for the sake of his body, that is, the church" (Col 1:24).

Initially it was in facing persecution that this theology of mystical union with the suffering Christ emerged in the New Testament and in the cult of the martyrs in the first centuries of the church; but it was soon transferred to any form of suffering, including the onset of disease and disability, when it was taught that God can use these as a means of drawing his people closer to himself in Jesus Christ.

Allied to this was the voluntary acceptance of personal suffering—notably fasting—as a means of discipline and spiritual growth. Asceticism has a long tradition, going back to pre-Christian days, as a form of spiritual training where the body is made to undergo discomforts and deprivations in order to release its grip on the spirit of man. Comparing himself to an athlete, Paul wrote: "But I pommel my body and subdue it, lest after preaching to others I myself should be disqualified" (1 Cor 9:27).

Since there flows from the cross the revelation that salvation involves both suffering and healing, both continue in the church's ministry as she proclaims the gospel. This does not answer the problem of why our prayers for the sick do not always seem to be heard, but it refutes the kind of explanations which are sometimes bandied about when the ministry of healing appears to fail ("We didn't have enough faith," or, "He learned so much through it"—those Old Testament concepts of suffering before they were transfigured by the passion of Jesus Christ).

The mystery remains of how God himself became totally involved in our human condition, including our suffering and death, to win for us his salvation through his Son. The problem of those who are not healed lies somewhere within the penumbra of that mystery.

You cannot tell a sick person this. Lying in a hospital bed in post-operative pain, or dragging oneself around crippled with arthritis year after wearying year, are not usually experiences of profound spiritual significance! Mental illness, too, brings its own tortures. To be gripped by a phobia which keeps you from the simplest everyday activities is dehumanizing in the extreme. To be told in such circumstances to offer your sufferings to the Lord can be anything but encouraging!

Yet those who continue to suffer, even after receiving ministry for healing, are often led by the Holy Spirit to see their commitment to Jesus Christ in a new light. The cross becomes central to their experience as it never did before. The approach of death can be a time of profound awareness of God's presence and saving love.

When we witness such manifestations of God's grace in those who are sick, the question about why they have not been cured in answer to prayer shrinks in significance. We know we are witnessing God's healing at a much deeper and more enduring level.

THREE

Gifts and Signs

N EARLY ONE FIFTH OF THE TEXT of the Gospels deals with Jesus'
healing ministry and the discussions caused by it. The
evangelists recorded that he healed on forty-one occasions, of which
thirty-three refer to physical infirmities. There were healings of
individuals and groups, and there were healings in crowds. The deaf,
dumb, blind, and paralytic came to him for healing; so did those with
leprosy, dropsy, fevers, and hemorrhages. Some were delivered from
evil spirits. He restored the ear of the servant Malchus after Peter had
sliced it off with a sword. And—most miraculously of all—he raised
three from the dead.

Jesus did not exercise his healing ministry as a means of drawing
attention to himself. He rejected the temptation to use his miraculous powers as a spectacle when the devil put it to him in the
wilderness (Mt 4:5-7; Lk 4:9-12). His healings usually followed his
preaching of the gospel, and he often urged those he healed privately
to keep the news to themselves. He refused to use the healing
ministry as a means of satisfying others' curiosity (Mk 8:11-13), and
those who were cured he pointed towards his heavenly Father rather
than to himself.

Yet the healings revealed him as the Messiah-Savior for whom
Israel had hoped. In his sermon in the synagogue at Nazareth, he
chose as his Scripture reading one of the great messianic passages of
Isaiah: "The Spirit of the Lord is upon me, / because he has anointed
me to preach good news to the poor. / He has sent me to proclaim
release to the captives / and recovering of sight to the blind, / to set

at liberty those who are oppressed, / to proclaim the acceptable year of the Lord" (Lk 4:18-19). The passage (Is 61:1-2; 58:6) originated in an oracular declaration that after the Babylonian exile the people of Israel would once again be free to return to Jerusalem and celebrate the year of Jubilee (Lev 25:10). According to the law of Moses, this was a year for the release of outstanding debts and certain social obligations, but by the time of Christ it was interpreted as a prophecy of the messianic age. In appealing to this text, Jesus was making the prodigious claim that he came as the Anointed One of God and that his Messiahship would be manifested, among other things, in the healings which he performed. He referred to the prophecy again when John the Baptist sent disciples to enquire if he was the One who was to come (Lk 7:20-22).

The demons whom Jesus exorcised recognized him. "I know who you are, the Holy One of God." shrieked the evil spirit which possessed the man in the synagogue at Capernaum (Lk 4:34); "You are the Son of God!" shouted the demons among the crowds (Lk 4:41). With their supernatural insight they penetrated the true explanation of Christ's extraordinary authority. They saw that Jesus was the Messiah and that he had come to set up God's kingdom, which meant the end of their dominion.

The disciples, too, realized that in Christ they walked with one who was closer to God than anyone they had ever known. Peter was the first to confess his belief that Jesus was the Messiah (Mk 8:29). After the death, resurrection, and ascension of Christ, and the gift of the Holy Spirit, the apostles and their immediate successors struggled to express the unheard-of claim, which they themselves would once have regarded as blasphemous had they not met Jesus, that God had indeed visited and redeemed his people. The one it was unlawful for a Jew to name had taken the name of "Emmanuel" ("God with us"). "For in Him the whole fulness of deity dwells bodily" (Col 2:9) was one Pauline expression of this revelation; "he was in the form of God" (Phil 2:6) was another. There are other texts in the books of the New Testament which attempt to teach how all of God that could take on human expression had been expressed in Jesus. It was out of these texts that the church was led to define the central Christian doctrine of the incarnation of the Son of God.

And the healing ministry of Christ was a dramatic manifestation of this truth. He spread healing around wherever he went because God was in him, recreating what he had made, making women and men who came to him a new people.

That ministry has been commented on and expounded many times, and I do not intend to repeat what can be read elsewhere. Rather, I would like to discuss Christ's treatment of the sick in a way which will help us to understand the renewal of the church's healing ministry in our own time.

To do this, I shall pick out certain characteristics in the stories of the healings as they have come down to us in the Gospels to show that Jesus' ministry was one of (1) pastoral care, (2) sacramental signs, and (3) charismatic power. I will explain what I mean by these categories in the following pages; but I want to emphasize that, although I have listed them as separate categories, they are in reality only different aspects of the one mission of Christ. The differentiation only has any value if it helps us to discern more clearly what God wants of us now.

1. A Ministry of Pastoral Care

At the heart of the new covenant is the revelation that "God so loved the world that he gave his only Son, that whoever believes in him should not perish but have eternal life" (Jn 3:16). Various biblical images convey this concept of divine love. The most vivid is that of God as our Father, who listens to his children and grants their requests (Mt 7:11; Lk 11:13). But for our purposes the image of God as the good shepherd is very vivid. In the Old Testament, God was regarded as the shepherd of Israel who healed their injuries (Ez 34:16). When Christ claimed to be the good shepherd who was willing to lay down his life for the sheep, he was attributing to himself the loving and caring attitude of God towards his people. We might say that one characteristic of Jesus' healing ministry was that it demonstrated the shepherding or pastoral love of God.

In the Gospels we catch glimpses of this pastoral care in Christ's reactions to the cases of sickness which he encountered. He had pity on the leper (Mk 1:41) and on the two blind men (Mt 20:34). He had compassion on the multitudes who brought their relatives and friends to him for healing (Mt 14:14). He was angry at the callousness of the Pharisees, who were more concerned to see if he would break the law on the sabbath than to see if he would cure a man with a withered hand (Mk 3:5). In the parable of the good Samaritan, the feelings of Christ himself are reflected in the pity that the traveler had on the injured man by the wayside (Lk 10:33). Jesus was concerned that the lepers he healed should be able to resume normal life among their families and neighbors, so he instructed them to have their cures officially certified (Lk 5:14; 17:14).

But the love of God is not restricted to those who are bound to him by the covenant. Israel had to learn that God's love and mercy reached out to women and men of other nations, too. Similarly, Jesus' disciples had to learn the boundlessness of God's love through seeing their Teacher heal Gentiles—the servant of the centurion (Mt 8:5-7), the daughter of the Syrophoenician woman (Mk 7:24-30), and the leper who was a Samaritan (Lk 17:11-19). No nation or group had an exclusive claim to the healing grace of God. Because Christ's healings were not sideshows to his mission but signs of the kingdom he announced, the offer of salvation was made to women and men of every place and every age.

Because they were signs of the kingdom, healings which left sin in control of a person were not true signs. God loves the sinner but rejects his sin. Jesus did not echo the Old Testament teaching that sickness and suffering in a person's life are the consequences of his personal sins. When the disciples asked if the man blind from birth was suffering because of his own sins or those of his parents, Christ refuted the suggestion (Jn 9:1-3). But he recognized that both personal and corporate sin can expose women and men to suffering and sickness, and that repentance and forgiveness go hand in hand with healing. To be "saved" in its fullest sense we must turn away from sin, put our trust in Jesus as our healer, and enter into a healthful relationship of sons and daughters with God through Christ. In the New Testament this is being "born again" (Jn 3:3), crossing "from death to life" (Jn 5:24), finding "eternal life" (Jn 6:40), believing "in the Lord Jesus" (Acts 16:31), coming to "peace with God through [faith in] our Lord Jesus Christ" (Rom 5:1), being made "a new creation [in Christ]" (2 Cor 5:17), putting off "the old nature . . . and [putting] on the new nature" (Col 3:9-10), and so on—all expressions with powerful healing overtones.

The healing of the paralyzed man manifested the love of God in forgiveness as well as in a physical cure. When he was lowered to the feet of Jesus, the Lord did not immediately pronounce the man healed. First he said to him, "My son, your sins are forgiven." The teachers of the law, hearing these words, accused Christ of blasphemy. Only God can forgive sins: "I will forgive their iniquity, and I will remember their sin no more" (Jer 31:34). But then, to prove that he had the power to forgive sins—or, as the author of Hebrews might have said, to show that he was "the author of salvation"—Jesus directed the paralyzed man to take up his bed and walk (Mk 2:1-12).

So the healings were dramatic presentations of the substance and essential meaning of Jesus' public ministry. They were manifesta- tions of God's loving care for his people, Jew and Gentile. They portrayed his message: "The time is fulfilled, and the kingdom of God is at hand; repent, and believe in the gospel" (Mk 1:15). They showed that the Old Testament prophecies of God's loving kindness and mercy were being fulfilled. The time of waiting was over, the messianic age for which Israel had hoped so long had arrived, the sovereign rule of God over his people was beginning.

The healings were challenges to those who received them and to those who witnessed them: were they willing to turn away from their sinful lives and accept the gospel, entering into the salvation which God offers through Jesus Christ?

2. A Ministry of Sacramental Signs

Jesus healed through the words he spoke, through the gestures he made, and through the things he used. If we adopt the old catechetical definition of a sacrament as "an outward and visible sign of the inward and spiritual grace," then we might say that the gestures and the things together with the words gave Christ's healing ministry a sacramental character.

In Christ the Word of God was not only a means of revelation; it was also a communication of authority. What Jesus commanded, happened. This is how God's Word is effective. "My word . . . shall accomplish that which I purpose, /and prosper in the thing for which I sent it" (Is 55:11). The story of the creation of the world tells how God spoke and what he said came to be. That same authority is evident in the effect Christ's words had on the sick: "Be clean," he said to the man with leprosy; "I say to you, rise," to the paralytic; "Stretch out your hand," to the man with the withered hand. They did, and immediately they were healed (Mk 1:41; 2:11; 3:5). Similarly, the demons were evicted when he spoke: "Come out of the man, you unclean spirit!" (Mk 5:8).

Jesus also healed by touch. He reached out his hand to the sick, like the leper (Mt 8:3: that was particularly significant, for in the Law Christ had made himself unclean by doing this). He touched the sick part of the body, like the eyes of the two blind men (Mt 9:29). Usually the touch was accompanied by a word of command, but occasionally only the touch was mentioned, as in the healing of Peter's mother-in-law (Mk 1:31 and Mt 8:15; Lk 4:39 says Christ rebuked the fever). Sometimes folk were healed when they touched him, like the woman with the hemorrhage and the sick among the crowds (Mk 5:28-9 and 6:56).

There are various references to the laying on of hands, suggesting a more formal gesture than a touch. Jairus asked Jesus to lay hands on his dying daughter (Mk 5:23). Christ laid hands on the sick with various kinds of diseases and on the woman with the spirit of infirmity (Lk 4:40 and 13:13).

The laying on of hands occurs in various contexts in the Old Testament. It was used in blessings, in the offering of sacrifices, in induction to an office, and in commissioning to a special task. There is no reference to its use in healing. Behind it is the idea of a transference of blessing or authority from one person to another, as when Moses laid hands on Joshua to give public witness to God's appointment of Joshua as Israel's leader (Nm 27:18, 23). Out of this arose the concept of God's hand as a sign of his Spirit (Ez 8:3). Particular importance was attached to the hand as a part of the whole, as a substitute for the person and the activities of the person to whom the hand belonged. Thus another version of the creation story attributed it to the work of God's hand ("My hand laid the foundation of the earth, / and my right hand spread out the heavens" [Is 48:13]). Similarly it was God's hand that led the people out of Egypt and smote their captors (Ex 7:4). When Jesus laid hands on a sick person for healing, therefore, he was using a sign that evoked a rich scriptural theme of God's presence and power.

He used other signs as well. When he came to the border of the Decapolis, he spat and touched the tongue of the deaf-mute and put his fingers in the man's ears, saying, "*Ephphatha!* Be opened!" (Mk 7:33-34). He spat on the eyes of the blind man of Bethsaida (Mk

8:23), and he made mud with his spittle to put on the eyes of the man born blind (Jn 9:6). Twice the sick were made to do something practical in order to effect their healing—the man born blind had to wash in the pool of Siloam, and the man with the withered arm had to hold it out towards Christ.

There is no record that Jesus himself used oil as a sign of healing. Perhaps that would have been inappropriate, since he was in his own person God's "Anointed One." But the twelve whom he sent out used oil (Mk 6:13). The use of oil and wine was common in medical practice (e.g., the parable of the good Samaritan), and spittle was believed to have healing properties (e.g., we still instinctively suck our finger when we cut it). Christ thus associated his healing work with that of the physicians of the time—a lesson his followers have had to relearn in most ages since. The lepers who were healed were told to show themselves to the priests to obtain the usual certificate of cleansing—the healing was genuine and verifiable according to contemporary medical thinking.

And Jesus identified himself with the healing role of the physician: "Those who are well have no need of a physician, but those who are sick; I came not to call the righteous, but sinners" (Mk 2:17).

The sacramental characteristic of Jesus' healing ministry, then, stemmed from his nature as the incarnate Word of God. Through the human body of Jesus, God manifested himself in a unique union with mankind. Those who heard Jesus speak and who saw him act, heard and saw God himself in human terms. The words Christ said to the sick, the gestures he employed, and the created things he involved, were outward and visible signs that God was reaching out through his creation to the sick in forgiveness, in deliverance, in healing, and in renewal—or their final salvation.

3. A Ministry of Charismatic Power

The authority which Jesus received from his Father was exercised with divine power. When people heard his preaching of the gospel and experienced forgiveness, healing, and release from evil spirits, they marvelled. "We have never experienced anything like this!" was their frequent reaction.

The source of Jesus' authority was the Holy Spirit, given at his baptism in the river Jordan. The voice of the Father proclaimed him to be God's Son, and the Spirit descended on him in bodily form. From there, "full of the Holy Spirit" (Lk 4:1), he went into the desert to do battle with Satan, resisting the temptations to use his power for the devil's purposes. Then he commenced his public ministry manifesting his authority in what he said and did.

What the public ministry demonstrated was that Jesus was able to exercise his authority in the power of the Spirit because he was completely submissive to the will of the Father in every situation he encountered. Although this is implicit in the synoptic Gospels, it is made explicit in the fourth Gospel. Many times in the Gospel of John there are references to Christ's obedience. "My father is working still, and I am working.... Truly, truly I say to you, the Son can do ... only what he sees the Father doing; for whatever he does, that the Son does likewise" (Jn 5:17, 19). Just before the greatest healing of all in this Gospel—the raising of Lazarus—Jesus prayed: "Father, I thank thee that thou hast heard me" (Jn 11:41). The work of salvation for which the Father sent the Son into the world springs from this perfect union between the Father and the Son.

From this unity of the Father and the Son comes the power of the Holy Spirit, and it is in this power that the miracles of healing are performed. In the synoptic Gospels, especially in Luke, "Spirit" and "power" become almost interchangeable words. "The power of the Lord was with him to heal" is noted in one passage (Lk 5:17); in another, Jesus is described as being conscious of power going out of him (Lk 8:46).

An interesting comparison can be made between the accounts of the controversy about casting out demons in Luke 11:20 and Matthew 12:28. Luke's version looks back to the Old Testament concept of God's power being like the exercise of a man's finger (implying that, marvelous though that divine power might be, it is puny compared with what God can really do when he gets going!): "If it is by the finger of God that I cast out demons, then the kingdom of God has come upon you." Matthew, on the other hand, records the saying in a slightly different form: "If it is by the Spirit of God that I cast out demons, then the kingdom of God has come upon you."

The operation of the Holy Spirit was associated in the New Testament with the coming of the kingdom of God, both as present in the ministry of Jesus Christ and of those who believed in him, and as a promise for the future of which healings and exorcisms were prophetic signs. When God rules in our hearts, then his Spirit can work powerfully through us. Christ held out the promise of the Father to his disciples as a fresh empowering to equip them to fulfill God's will, to uphold them in persecutions, and to guide them. This power was not a disembodied magical energy which could be passed on to others as a favor. That was the error of Simon, the sorcerer of Samaria (Acts 8:19). Rather, this was the power of God's presence and grace, and its operation in the lives of the disciples depended on their complete obedience to the Father, too.

Jesus' healings and exorcisms were vivid demonstrations that the kingdom of darkness was being banished by the kingdom of light. "Now shall the ruler of this world be cast out," he announced (Jn 12:31). Those who refused to recognize the signs of divine triumph in the spiritual warfare were in grave danger of being imprisoned by evil forever. When the teachers of the law from Jerusalem accused Jesus of driving out demons through the power of Beelzebub, he warned them they were verging on the sin of blasphemy against the Holy Spirit (Mk 3:29). Such a sin becomes unforgivable because to deny God's goodness in the face of the clearest indications of that goodness is to be spiritually blind and incapable of receiving God's light.

But to be rid of evil and healed of sickness is not enough. We also need the gift of the Holy Spirit; otherwise the spiritual vacuum left by the departure of Satan is as vulnerable as an empty house is to burglars (Mt 12:43-45). Sickness may not be caused directly by our own sinfulness, but persistence in sin makes our healing incomplete; we are not fully open to the saving grace of which it is a sign. The man who was healed at the pool of Bethesda was warned to stop sinning lest something worse happened to him (Jn 5:14).

The healing ministry of Jesus was charismatic in two senses: it was an operation of the Holy Spirit through his own person and it was a gift of the Holy Spirit to the one who was healed. That is why so often their response was praise of God and faith in Jesus. Only the Holy Spirit could give them that.

The Response of Faith

Any movement of God towards us has to be appropriated by faith, and in the New Testament faith is frequently mentioned as a factor in the healing process. Not that the healing of a person ultimately depended on their faith or the faith of anyone else, but rather faith was present in some degree among those involved. The leper had faith to ask for cleansing (Mk 1:40); the woman with the hemorrhage was commended by Jesus for her faith (Mk 5:34); the two blind men believed Christ could heal them (Mt 9:28), and so did the ten lepers (Lk 17:13). The faith of the centurion who sent a message to Christ asking him to heal his servant roused Jesus' admiration (Lk 7:7), and also the nobleman whose son was sick in Capernaum (Jn 4:47). Christ noticed the faith of the four men who brought their paralyzed friend to him on a stretcher (Mk 2:3), and the faith of the Syrophoenician woman who came to him on behalf of her daughter (Mt 15:28).

"All things are possible to him who believes," said Jesus, after his disciples had failed to cure the boy with the evil spirit. "I believe," cried the boy's father, "help my unbelief!" (Mk 9:23-24). What he seems to have been saying is, "Help me, for such belief as I have must be counted as incomplete in comparison with what is demanded" (a sentiment shared by everyone who engages in the church's ministry of healing!) In other words, even faith itself is a gift from God.

Yet sometimes faith seemed to be absent. The man born blind was healed without any request on his part, although he later confessed his faith in Jesus Christ (Jn 9:38). The man who was healed at the pool of Bethesda did not appear to have any faith (Jn 5:7), and the crowds who brought their sick to Jesus often seemed to be acting from a vague notion about a wonder-worker rather than out of faith in God. What the Gospels reveal is that God acts according to his sovereign will, not according to the degree or even presence of faith in the persons involved. He has mercy on whom he has mercy. Faith in Jesus Christ brings the sick into a relationship with God which enables him to act in and through their lives by his Spirit, but he is not dependent on their faith to do so.

On the other hand, a lack of faith can be a stumbling block to the operation of his grace. Mark and Matthew wrote that Jesus was unable to do more than a few miracles in his home town because they took offence at him (Mk 6:5; Mt 13:58). When the Holy Spirit works, the Father is glorified through Jesus Christ. In his healings, as in all other aspects of his ministry, the Son gave glory to the Father, and he told his disciples that the same Spirit would enable them to see God's glory in his ministry, too. So the accounts of the healings in the Gospels often end with the people praising God. A ministry of pastoral care, sacramental signs, and charismatic power directs the faith and love and hope of those who receive it to the source of all grace.

In Matthew's version of the healing of the paralyzed man, there is an additional phrase which forms a link between Jesus' healing ministry and that of the apostolic church: "When the crowds saw it, they were afraid, and they glorified God, *who had given such authority to men*" (Mt 9:8, my italics). The phrase could mean giving such authority to men in the person of Christ, but it is more likely the evangelist was thinking of the healing ministry continued in Christ's name by his disciples after his resurrection.

Jesus did not always have to be present when an invalid was healed. The centurion, the nobleman of Capernaum, and the Syrophoenician woman came to him about their sick servant, son, and daughter respectively, and he answered their requests with gifts of healing without visiting the sick themselves. Then his healing ministry was extended through those he sent out. The first group were the twelve disciples, to whom he gave authority to drive out evil spirits and heal every disease and sickness (Mt 10:1)— which they did, using olive oil (Mk 6:13). The second group were seventy disciples, whose success was such that they caused Jesus to rejoice in the Holy Spirit and offer a prayer of thanksgiving to the Father (Lk 10:21). It is noteworthy that he sent only those who were personally committed to him.

The sending of the twelve and the seventy foreshadowed the wider mission which was to be given to the church. In the last discourse in the fourth Gospel, Jesus made this promise: "Truly, truly, I say to you, he who believes in me will also do the works that I do; and greater works than these will he do, because I go to the Father. Whatever you ask in my name, I will do it, that the Father may be glorified in the Son; if you ask anything in my name, I will do it" (Jn 14:12-14).

The completion of Jesus' mission with the gift of the Holy Spirit was to inaugurate an age in which the works which had been focused on his person would now be experienced far and wide. This is the most likely interpretation of doing "greater works than these"— greater, that is, in the effect those works produce (there cannot be an intrinsically greater miracle than a healing or a raising from the dead). The works of Jesus had limited effect because they were experienced only by those who met him. Now the apostles and their successors were to spread that experience across different nations and into future ages.

Because of the gift of the Spirit, the power which Christ exercised would now be exercised by them, provided they asked in his name. To ask in his name does not mean to invoke the name of Jesus as a kind of magic spell; it means to ask as his representative while about his business. As Jesus had come in his Father's name (Jn 5:43), so he was sending his disciples out in his name. He had spread healing around wherever he had gone; now he was to spread it further through them. Thus would the Father and the Son be glorified through this greater work of the Holy Spirit.

Apostolic Ministry

Since the healing ministry of the apostolic church was a continuation of Jesus' own ministry to the sick, it had the same pastoral, sacramental, and charismatic characteristics. "The Lord worked with them and confirmed the message by the signs that attended it" (Mk 16:20).

The healings in Acts read like a second installment of those in the Gospels. There are five cases of individuals being healed through the ministry of Peter, John, and Paul (Acts 3:2; 9:32; 14:8; 16:18; 28:8) and two raisings of the dead, one by Peter and one by Paul (Acts 9:37; 20:9). There are general references to healing by the apostles (Acts 2:43; 15:12), by Stephen (6:8), by Philip (8:13) and by Paul and Barnabas (14:3; 15:12). Healings are noted in reference to Peter's shadow (Acts 5:15), Philip's preaching (8:7) and Paul's clothing (19:12). Ananias was involved in a ministry in which Paul was healed of blindness (Acts 9:17). Paul himself was healed from severe stoning (Acts 14:19) and protected from the effects of snakebite (28:3). Put together, these healings in Acts present a remarkable picture of the Spirit of Jesus (Acts 16:7) working in and through his people.

This picture is filled out in the details of each healing. The first to be described fully is that in Acts 3 and 4. The healing of the lame man at the Beautiful Gate of the temple reflects the ministry of Christ in the Gospels. Peter and John were going to the temple for one of the statutory times of daily prayer observed by devout Jews whether they were in Jerusalem or elsewhere. When the lame man begged for alms, Peter told him, "I have no silver and gold" (3:6). This may have been the literal truth: people in ancient times did not carry coins round with them to anything like the same extent as we do today.

"In the name of Jesus Christ of Nazareth, walk," Peter went on, taking the lame man by the right hand. The man leapt up and danced into the temple, praising God. The amazement of the crowd provided the apostle with an opportunity to preach the gospel, using the healing as visible evidence of the truth of what he was proclaiming, rather as Jesus had done after the healing of the paralyzed man. The Christ who had been crucified in Jerusalem only a few weeks previously had been raised from the dead by God as his Messiah: "And his name, by faith in his name, has made this man strong whom you see and know; and the faith which is through Jesus has given the man this perfect health in the presence of you all" (Acts 3:16).

Peter's opportunity was widened when he was taken before the Sanhedrin with John and the man who had been healed. Facing those who had been instrumental in bringing Jesus to trial before Pilate, he declared, "By the name of Jesus Christ of Nazareth, whom you crucified, whom God raised from the dead, by him this man is standing before you well" (Acts 4:10). Then he rounded off his speech saying that salvation in its widest sense could come to them in no other way: "And there is salvation in no one else, for there is no other name under heaven . . . by which we must be saved" (4:12).

It is a classic model for the ministry of healing, from the point of view of the church. Peter did what he could for the lame man (pastoral care); he had no alms to offer him, but in faith the apostle invoked a richer gift. He spoke authoritatively in the name of Christ and took the lame man by the hand (sacramental signs). The healing gift caused the man to leap up and praise God (charismatic power). The event filled the crowd with wonder and provided Peter with opportunities to proclaim the salvation (full healing) of God.

Further healings described by Luke in Acts underline different aspects of this ministry—repentance, faith, forgiveness, freedom from evil spirits, the infilling of the Holy Spirit. And still we are conscious that, through the healings, Jesus himself is working to reveal the glory of the Father. Acts is often called the gospel of the

Holy Spirit, and in these stories we become vividly aware of the Spirit's operation in taking what is Christ's and making it known to his disciples (Jn 16:14). The church—through one, two, or more of its members—becomes the body of Christ in what we might crudely call a very tangible and audible manner: the words and gestures of its members are the words and gestures of the Head of the church in the experience of the sick and demon-possessed.

After his encounter with the risen Christ on the road to Damascus, Saul had to await the arrival of Ananias before he was healed. For him recovery of sight was a symbol of his baptism, his enlightening from a blindness which had been spiritual as well as physical. Ananias ministered to him through the laying on of hands: "Brother Saul, the Lord Jesus who appeared to you on the road by which you came, has sent me that you may regain your sight and be filled with the Holy Spirit" (Acts 9:17).

Peter spoke to Aeneas in Lydda as Jesus spoke to the paralyzed man: "Jesus Christ heals you; rise and make your bed" (Acts 9:34). He then went on to raise Dorcas (9:40) as Christ had gone on to raise the daughter of the ruler of the synagogue (Mk 5:35 ff). Paul healed a cripple at Lystra with a similar word of command, among the miracles and wonders he performed with Barnabas in the province of Galatia (Acts 14:8-10).

Again, the deliverance of the slave girl in Philippi echoes Christ's exorcism of the demoniac (Lk 8:28). The evil spirits in the slave girl also had supernatural powers of detection; they recognized who Paul and Silas really were: "These men are servants of the Most High God, who proclaim to you the way of salvation." The apostles invoked the source of their authority: "I charge you in the name of Jesus Christ to come out of her" (Acts 16:16-18).

The danger of taking the Lord's name in vain was shown through the incident of the sons of Sceva. These Jewish exorcists tried to copy the apostles, but their lack of faith was made obvious in the words with which they addressed the evil spirit: "I adjure you by the Jesus whom Paul preaches." The phrase, "whom Paul preaches," gave their game away: they were not committed to that name personally. The evil spirit saw through their trick: "Jesus I know, and Paul I know; but who are you?" The man possessed by the evil spirit then attacked them so violently that they had to flee wounded and with torn clothes (Acts 19:13-16).

On Malta Paul healed, through prayer and the laying on of hands, the father of Publius, the chief official (Acts 28:7-8). In Jerusalem the people brought the sick into the street so that Peter's shadow might fall on some of them as he passed by (5:15). And in Philippi Paul's sweat-rag and leather apron, which he used in his trade as a tentmaker, became the means of healing for those who were diseased or possessed by evil spirits (19:12).

Apostolic Teaching

The Jewish and Hellenistic world into which the church's healing ministry came was one in which cures were already sought in different ways. Much that passed for medicine was sheer superstition or magic. But not all. Among the Jews, the law of Moses contained sensible directions about hygiene and sanitation, and simple local treatments were prescribed, as when Isaiah advised a cake of figs to be used as a poultice for King Hezekiah (2 Kgs 20:7). Uniquely among ancient peoples, the Jews separated the practice of primitive medicine from the role of the priest, except in certifying the cure of cases like leprosy. Where such medicine was tainted with magic, Judaism reacted against it, which is probably why Asa was condemned for consulting doctors (2 Chr 16:12).

Through the influence of Greek culture, the Jews came to recognize medical skill as a gift from God: "Honor the physician with the honor due him, according to your need of him, for the Lord created him; for healing comes from the Most High. . . . The Lord created medicines from the earth, and a sensible man will not despise them" (Sir 38:1-2, 4). It was, therefore, no problem for Christians from a Jewish background to accept the ministry of a Greek like Luke, once the Greeks were admitted to the church without first being made Jews. Luke's interest and skill in medicine made a unique contribution to his Gospel. Of all the evangelists, he shows a special care in recording the healing miracles of Christ (and on one occasion deleted from the story of the woman with a hemorrhage Mark's implied criticism of doctors—compare Luke 8:43 with Mark 5:26).

Luke did not work out a theology of the ministry of healing. In the Book of Acts he let the story of the apostolic mission demonstrate how the Lord worked with and through the infant church, the healings becoming powerful visual aids to the gospel. They were proof that Jesus had been raised from the dead (Acts 3:15 and 4:10) and that divine power was given to those who ministered in Jesus' name (14:3). But in telling the story he revealed that the infant church's concept of God was already developing beyond the Jewish monotheism within which Christianity was born. Like other New Testament authors, Luke recognized a relationship between God as Father and God as Spirit which was complementary to his understanding of Jesus as the Son of God. He made it clear that the power which effects the healings asked for in Jesus' name was the power of the Spirit of God, and more than any other evangelist he saw the age of salvation as the age of the Spirit.

So he presented Jesus as the Spirit-anointed Servant of God, prophesied in Isaiah, who calls together and sends out in the power of the Spirit the new people of God; the church herself is the community of the Spirit foretold by Joel ("I will pour out my Spirit on all flesh") proclaiming the gospel of the kingdom with signs following. For Luke everything that happened in the life of the church in one way or another was inspired, controlled, and fulfilled by the Spirit, because every member of the church was endowed with the Spirit and therefore equipped to exercise divine power in Jesus' name. The healings were but one aspect of the church's life and mission.

It was Paul who analyzed more closely just how the Holy Spirit worked through the Christian in the church. For this apostle, to be united with the Lord in baptism is to be washed, justified, and sanctified "in the name of the Lord Jesus Christ and in the Spirit of our God" (1 Cor 6:11): that is, to be cleansed from sin, to be set in a right relationship with God, and to be one who constantly receives the Holy Spirit, who changes us into the holy people God wills us to be. Through baptism we are initiated into the body of Christ. By sharing his Spirit with those whom God calls into the church, Christ diffuses his ministry, including his healing ministry, throughout his community.

Paul used various words to describe this diffusion of the Spirit among the members of the church—"ministries," "powers," but the most common one was "spiritual gifts" (Greek, *charisma, charismata*). These charisms are most varied because the tasks the church has to perform are also varied. In the fellowship of believers we have to learn that others' gifts and the tasks they are called to perform may be different from ours. In any case, charisms are not personal possessions; they are signs of God's activity in and through his people. Nor are they marks of personal sanctity; God can use anyone for his purpose as he wills, even those who do not acknowledge him.

Among these spiritual gifts Paul listed "gifts of healing" (1 Cor 12:9). Further on in the same chapter he included those who are given power to heal in a catalogue of different ministries resulting from spiritual gifts: apostles, prophets, teachers, those who perform miracles, those who are given power to heal. The list also includes helpers, administrators, those who speak in tongues, and those who interpret tongues (1 Cor 12:28-30). We have no means of knowing what the difference was between those who perform miracles and those who are given power to heal. Perhaps some through a gift of faith (verse 9) were equipped to do amazing things in the cause of the gospel far beyond the ministry of healing the sick. What the apostle emphasizes is that the ministry of healing is the work of God in the church through its members; it is not a power which is theirs but is Christ's, manifested by the Holy Spirit for the benefit of the whole church and its mission.

Paul did not answer the question: Do natural gifts of healing come from God? But we may deduce from what he taught that no *Christian* action in ministry to others is independent of the Holy Spirit, no matter what label we attach to it. He would have been suspicious of anything "fleshly," for that was tainted with sin, but he would probably have said that skills used for the glory of God are manifestations of the Holy Spirit.

Apostolic teaching and practice come together in the famous passage about the healing ministry in James 5:13-16: "Is any one among you suffering? Let him pray. Is any cheerful? Let him sing praise. Is any among you sick? Let him call the elders of the church, and let them pray over him, anointing him with oil in the name of the Lord; and the prayer of faith will save the sick man, the Lord will raise him up; and if he has committed sins, he will be forgiven. Therefore confess your sins to one another, and pray for one another, that you may be healed."

The prayer of the elders was the primary element in the ministry. The healing grace of God was to be expected in response to their prayer. Although the use of olive oil was assumed, there was no reference to the laying on of hands. This was such a surprising omission that an early commentator, Origen, read the text as "Call the elders, and let them lay their hands on him anointing him with oil." The relationship between healing and the forgiveness of sins was believed to be so close that the sick person was to confess his sins to another so that prayer for forgiveness could be offered as well.

So the healing ministry of Jesus Christ continued in the apostolic church after his resurrection, manifesting the love of God and proclaiming the reality of his kingdom among women and men everywhere. In the next chapter we shall briefly trace how that ministry has continued through the centuries down to our own times.

But before we leave the evidence of the New Testament, it is worth noting that, unlike Christ's ministry, that of the apostles does not appear to have been one hundred percent successful. Paul, as we have seen, had a thorn in the flesh—perhaps an illness,—which was not removed after he had prayed about it (2 Cor 12:7-10); he was ill for some time in Galatia, perhaps with an eye infection (Gal 4:13-16); Trophimus was so ill that he had to be left behind at Miletus (2 Tm 4:20); Epaphroditus was so ill that he almost died (Phil 2:26-27); and Timothy had a persistent stomach complaint for which Paul prescribed wine (1 Tm 5:23).

FOUR

Help in Ages Past

W E HAVE IDENTIFIED IN THE HEALING MINISTRY of Jesus Christ and in that of the New Testament church characteristics which I have catalogued as pastoral, sacramental, and charismatic. As I said, these distinctions must not be pressed too far; the Spirit of God is active in pastoral care and sacramental signs as well as charismatic power. But I would like to continue with them, for they will help us to discern how a proper restoration of that ministry depends in part on bringing together what the church has put asunder.

In this chapter I shall sketch the development of the church's ministry to the sick across the centuries under these three categories. The illustrations I shall use should be regarded rather like those clips from films which appear in TV documentaries. They cannot be regarded as serious history because they are so few; but they give a background to the topic and set it in some sort of perspective. A general picture of the past helps us to understand more clearly the situation we are in at present. It also checks the all-too-common assumption in some circles where the ministry of healing is practiced that the Holy Spirit was dormant in this field from the close of the apostolic era to the beginning of our own.

A Pastoral Ministry

The early Christians recognized that the redeeming work of God in Jesus Christ had brought a new healing power into the world which manifested the love of God for his people, and as disciples of the Good Shepherd they had a special concern for the sick. They did not abandon what they knew about health and healing from the Bible and from their own culture. Rather, the light of the gospel enabled them gradually to reject what was magical or idolatrous about the medical practices they were familiar with and to incorporate what they believed to be of God into their own pastoral care. Hence from the beginning there was a close connection between the church's ministry to the sick and the work of physicians.

In the second century, Cosmas and Damien were respected for their work in the city of Rome as Christian doctors. They were known as "the moneyless ones" because they practiced medicine among the poor without charging a fee for their services. Long afterwards a hall in the Roman Forum was taken over as a church and dedicated in their honor. This church has always had a special association with the ministry of healing.

The care of the sick was a feature of Christian life which was noticed by the pagan world. Although medicine was practiced in the Greek and Roman civilizations, it was largely for the benefit of the wealthy. Those who were diseased among the poor were lucky indeed if anyone took the trouble to look after them.

When Alexandria was devastated by an outbreak of plague in the middle of the third century, Dionysius, the bishop of the church in that city, described the devotion with which the Christians tended the sick, often catching the plague and dying of it themselves in consequence. This contrasted with their pagan neighbors, who either threw their sick relatives into the street or fled from the city, leaving those with the plague to die.

Bishops used church buildings as hospitals in times of emergency. From this there sprang the idea of building separate accommodation for the sick near to the church. Basil (d. 379), Bishop of Caesarea in Cappadocia and one of the leading theologians of the church in the East, is regarded as a pioneer of the Christian hospital movement. A few years before his death he built, around his basilica, houses for physicians and nurses as well as accommodation for the aged and the sick. His example was copied elsewhere.

The establishment of the religious orders was an important factor in the spread of hospitals and in the growth of nursing care. In 529 Benedict of Nursia founded a monastery with a hospital attached at Monte Cassino in southern Italy. His rule directed that "the care of the sick must be attended to before all things." The Benedictine pattern was followed by other orders. When we visit monasteries and convents today (or the ruins of medieval houses) we find the *infirmarium* built near to the church and on the sunny and sheltered side of the complex. Some *infirmaria* had wards with beds on either side and an altar at one end so that patients could hear mass and receive communion without being moved. Monasteries had their own herb gardens for medicinal purposes, and their hygienic arrangements were far in advance of what was common in secular life.

The monastic *infirmaria* were originally intended for members of their own community, but the hospitality offered by the religious orders meant that their facilities became available for sick pilgrims and invalids from the neighborhood. What might be called an out-patients' room was provided along with a separate hospice for long-stay patients. Some orders began to specialize in the care of the sick, including the provision of isolation wards for those with leprosy (known as "lazar houses" from the old French *lazar* meaning "leper," derived from the name of Lazarus).

The twelfth century saw an increase in the number of hospitals founded in cathedral cities and staffed by religious. They included St. John's Hospital, Canterbury (118); Holy Cross Hospital, Winchester (1132); St. Bartholomew's Hospital, London (1137); St. Thomas' Hospital, London (1215); and St. Mary's Hospital, London (1179). The latter became the Hospital of St. Mary of Bethlehem or "Bedlam": it was later to specialize in the care of mental cases.

The needs of pilgrims led to the foundation of various new religious orders. One of these was the Order of St. John of Jerusalem, founded in 1099 with the task of caring for those who made pilgrimages to the Holy Land. This order established hospitals in Jerusalem and on the islands of Rhodes and Malta.

But it was the women's orders which did most to develop hospital care. The Sisters of St. Catherine of Siena and the Sisters of St.

Elizabeth of Hungary are but two of the large number of women's orders which specialize in nursing even today. Some hospital traditions—the provision of chaplains and a chapel, the term "sister" (used in England), and the nurse's uniform—go back to the days when a hospital was part of a religious house.

The rise of the universities in the Middle Ages meant the appearance of medical departments staffed not only by clergy but also by laymen with a specialist interest in research into the functioning of the human body. This confronted the church with novel ethical problems. Was it right to dissect a corpse? Were herbal remedies of God or of the devil? The period saw a gradual hardening of the church's attitude towards medical research, and various councils of bishops banned their clergy from taking part in anatomical experiments.

During these centuries, the profession of the doctor slowly emerged alongside that of the clergyman. Throughout the Renaissance and the Reformation, the physician came to the fore as a man of learning and specialist competence. The foundation in the seventeenth and eighteenth centuries of various professional societies to monitor the training and careers of doctors and surgeons set the seal on this development. It also marked the beginning of a slow separation between the medical care of the sick and the pastoral ministry of the church.

This secularization of medical care was matched by a similar secularization of nursing care. The dissolution of the monasteries in Protestant Europe meant the closure of many hospitals. This, in turn, forced other bodies, such as city corporations or groups of benefactors, to found hospitals instead. The eighteenth century saw the beginning of the voluntary hospitals movement in Britain and North America, due largely to an awakened Christian conscience as the growth of industrial urban areas created health and welfare problems. Thomas Bond, a Quaker, started a fund for the establishment of the first hospital in the United States; his plan was supported by Benjamin Franklin, and the Pennsylvania Hospital in Philadelphia was opened in 1751.

In congregations outside large towns, the clergyman and his wife acted as physician and nurse when the occasion demanded. George

Herbert (1593-1633), the saintly priest-poet of the Church of England ("Teach me, my God and King," "King of glory, King of peace," "Let all the world in every corner sing") advised the clergy, in *The Country Parson*, to learn how to care for the sick. They should have at least one "book of physic" in their house and they should grow herbs for medicinal use in their garden: "Hyssop, valerian, mercury, adder's tongue, yerrow, melilot and St. John's-wort made into a salve; and elder, camomile, mallows, comphrey and smallage made into a poultice, have done great and rare cures." He also advised the parson and his wife, in ministering to the sick, not to forget to pray with them: "This raiseth the action from the shop to the church."

Even when the profession of the qualified doctor became established, a few clergy continued to combine both roles. One was the late Dr. Martin Lloyd-Jones, the influential preacher and writer. And, of course, medical work went with the missionaries to all parts of the world. Dr. Albert Schweitzer set up his hospital in Lambarene in what was then French Equatorial Africa in 1913. The histories of Christian missions are packed with the names of Christian doctors and nurses and other medical people who went as members of the church to establish hospitals, dispensaries, medical schools, and health centers in different lands.

The secularization of medical and nursing services has meant that the church's pastoral care of the sick has been narrowed down to the more general task of visiting them and looking after them in practical matters—little more than being a good neighbor. When this kind of pastoral care is offered without any sacramental or charismatic ministry, what the church does seems little more than what the sick might expect from any welfare agency. Indeed, sometimes our ministry to the sick has seemed just that!

But a restoration of that ministry on the model of the New Testament should work towards a closer cooperation with medical and nursing services, since they offer an important pastoral element in the ministry of healing. The healing for which the secular services work may not be as full and complete as a Christian believes healing can be, but where they promote the health and ultimate well-being of patients, we can discern in them the hand of God himself.

A Sacramental Ministry

The laying on of hands with prayer and the anointing of the sick developed into a sacramental and liturgical ministry in the early church. One of the first known Christian prayer books, the *Apostolic Tradition* of Hippolytus (from Rome in the third century), has a form for the blessing of oil to be used for the sick: "O God, who sanctifieth this oil, grant that it may give strength to all who taste of it and health to all who use it." From this it sounds as if the invalid was expected to drink the oil as well as be anointed with it. Although the anointing was normally done by the bishop or one of his presbyters, lay persons could exercise this function as well. Unlike some other sacramental ministries, it was never regarded as the sole preserve of the clergy.

Those who were seriously ill were prepared for the laying on of hands and anointing by confessing their sins, in accordance with the injunctions in James 5. The reconciliation of sinners to communion with the church—itself a separate liturgy—was adapted for the sick so that they could be assured of God's forgiveness. The service for the sick therefore consisted of Bible reading, prayer, confession and absolution, anointing, and communion.

In the early Middle Ages, however, this service came to be regarded not so much a ministry of healing as a preparation for death. Infant mortality was much higher than it is today, and people's life expectancy much shorter. Death was a regular visitor to all households. Scriptural teaching about healing tended to be associated with charismatic gifts rather than with sacramental ministrations. The desire to be assured of divine forgiveness became more urgent than the hope for divine healing. The liturgy for the sick became *unctio in extremis,* the "last rites," given after rather than before the final communion.

This distortion of the sacramental ministry to the sick was strengthened by the medieval theologians. Since they were only familiar with anointing as a preparation for death, this is how they analyzed it in their sacramental teaching. Unction became one of the seven sacraments of the church, instituted by Jesus Christ and the apostles as means through which Christians could be assured of God's grace; and the grace the theologians associated with anointing was the forgiveness of sins and strength to face the approach of death. Healing was relegated to the sidelines.

William of Auvergne (d. 1249), Bishop of Paris, was typical of these teachers. Writing about unction, he said, "Since those who are about to die are like the bride who is about to enter the chamber of the bridegroom, it is clear to men of understanding how necessary and fitting is the sacrament of last hallowing." The great Thomas Aquinas (d. 1274) said the purpose of unction was to prepare the soul for entrance into heaven. This concept of anointing has dominated the Roman Catholic church up until the middle of the present century.

Alongside this was the further belief that, except in very special cases, the gifts of healing recorded in the New Testament had been a particular dispensation from God in the early days of the gospel—"dispensationalism" as it came to be called. Augustine, Bishop of Hippo (d. 43), was an influential proponent of this doctrine, although he later changed his mind after experiencing healings in his own congregation.

The Reformers were more concerned to refute the contention that unction was a sacrament than to recover its scriptural function as a ministry of healing. Martin Luther (d. 1546) allowed that anointing could stimulate faith in the recipient and therefore help him to be more open to the forgiveness of God. John Calvin (d. 1564) agreed that Jesus had commissioned his disciples to heal the sick through anointing, and that James 5 showed oil was used in this way; but he regarded the ministry as unimportant because he believed that healing gifts had been withdrawn from the church:

> The gift of healing disappeared with the other miraculous powers which the Lord was pleased to give for a time, that it might render the new preaching of the gospel forever wonderful. Therefore, were we to grant that anointing was a sacrament of those powers which were then administered by the hands of the apostles, it pertains not to us, to whom no such powers have been committed.

Dispensationalism has remained a traditional conviction among some Protestants ever since. It is still powerful in certain schools of theology and constitutes one of the main sources of opposition to the restoration of the ministry of healing in the Christian church today.

Anglicans followed the teaching and practice of the continental Reformers. Anointing was dropped from the service for the visitation of the sick in the *Book of Common Prayer* and, as we have seen, they treated the invalid as one who was suffering for his sins. Most of them also adhered to dispensationalism. One quaint version of this belief was put forward by John Tillotson (d. 1694), Archbishop of Canterbury. He held that gifts of healing had been withdrawn from the church by God when Christianity became the established religion of the Roman Empire under the emperor Constantine.

Interestingly, in her response to the Reformation crisis, the Roman Catholic church did not entirely lose sight of the scriptural basis for the sacrament of unction. When the Council of Trent debated unction in 1551, the first draft of the decree followed the medieval theologians and declared that the sacrament should only be given "to those who are in their final struggle and who have come to grips with death and who are about to go forth to the Lord." But in the course of the debates, the Council changed the decree to read: "This anointing is to be used for the sick, but especially for those who are so dangerously ill as to appear at the point of departing this life."

Although both Roman Catholic and Protestant traditions seemed to reject the ministry of healing in their official formularies and liturgies, groups of Christians still sought Jesus Christ as a healer when they ministered to the sick. It was among the Non-Jurors that a sacramental ministry of anointing for healing reappeared in England. The Non-Jurors regarded themselves as the true Church of England after the accession of William and Mary in 1688. They had refused to take the oath of allegiance to the king, on the ground that by so doing they would break the previous oath to James II and his successors. Although only a small group, they survived until the end of the eighteenth century and exercised a considerable influence over Anglicans because their membership included a few learned and saintly people.

A service for the anointing of the sick for healing was included in the Non-Jurors' prayer books, published in 1718 and 1734. These services may have inspired the inclusion of a similar rite in the prayer book of the Episcopal Church in the United States. The example of the Non-Jurors was followed by Anglo-Catholics in the Church of England in the next century. It is true that these high churchmen were more concerned to restore anointing as one of the seven sacraments of Catholic antiquity rather than specifically as a ministry of healing; but among them were those who urged the Church of England to return to the scriptural practice of anointing the sick— not just those who were dying—and praying that they might be cured.

Belief in the direct healing power of God was prominent among the Holiness groups which sprang out of the evangelical revivals in the nineteenth century. The laying on of hands and anointing was practiced among these forerunners of the classic Pentecostal churches. We shall see in the next chapter how these influenced the current restoration of the church's ministry of healing. These Holiness groups certainly would not have regarded anointing as a sacrament like baptism or the Lord's Supper, as Roman Catholics and Anglo-Catholics did; but that did not prevent their believing that by their following the teaching of the New Testament, Jesus Christ would heal in their day as he had done during his earthly ministry. And their experiences confirmed them in that belief.

A Charismatic Ministry

Although belief in dispensationalism was widespread, gifts of healing were experienced in different ages and in different places throughout the Christian world, and these kept alive the hope that Jesus Christ's commission to his disciples was still relevant to the church.

Healings are often recounted in the lives of the saints. Modern editors of these lives, however, present us with a problem. They point out that miracle healings are part of the stock in trade of hagiography, and that such happenings do not stand up to forensic scrutiny. The tales are usually modelled on New Testament accounts, and they were included, say the editors, as a means of honoring the subject of their book and of emphasizing his or her holiness. They must not be regarded as factual history.

But we must not forget that nobody writes history objectively and that even the modern editor of the life of an early saint will interpret what he reads in the light of his own experience and expectation. If he belongs to a culture which automatically discounts the miraculous, then he will dismiss everything he reads as legendary—or he will argue that what were once regarded as miraculous cures would nowadays be recognized as scientifically possible.

When we look back at these stories today, however, not all of us can so easily dismiss them in this way. Our experience of the church's ministry of healing enables us to look through the hagiographic material to events which are not unlike what we see happening round us. We may need to demythologize the tales to some extent, but that does not mean we assume that in every case nothing extraordinary happened.

We must respect the integrity of chroniclers like Bede, the first historian of the English people. He, like most churchmen of his time, thought that healing gifts had been withdrawn from the church at the end of the apostolic age; yet he recorded stories of cures in the ministries of Christian leaders in Saxon Britain. Bede is remarkable in the trouble he took to collect information about his subject, meticulously listing his sources and separating fact from hearsay. We have no reason to suppose that, when he recounted a miraculous healing, there was no core of historical truth behind it.

One of the great church leaders in the north of England whom Bede admired was John of Beverley (d. 721), a monk of Whitby and then Bishop of York. Bede almost certainly knew John personally. Bede records in his *History* that many miracles were told of John by those who knew him, in particular by Berthrun, formerly John's deacon and, after the bishop's death, abbot of Beverley. Bede described Berthrun as "a most reverend and truthful man" and said he would relate only a few of the stories he had heard from John's colleague.

One concerned a young man who was unable to speak and whose head was so covered in scabs that no hair grew on it. John took the youth into his community and one day in Lent prayed with him, making the sign of the cross on the youth's tongue. Then the bishop ordered him to say *gae* (the early English word for yes). This the youth did. Quite soon afterwards the young man was learning letters and syllables from the bishop. "All those who were present say that all that day and the next night, as long as he could keep awake, the youth never stopped saying something, and expressing his own thoughts and wishes to others, which he had never been able to do so previously."

But it was only the youth's dumbness that was healed at first. The bishop sent for a physician to look at the scabs. The bishop then prayed for the youth and blessed him. Soon afterwards his skin was healed and his hair began to grow vigorously.

Bede concluded:

> the youth obtained a clear complexion, readiness of speech, and a beautiful head of hair, whereas he had formerly been deformed, destitute, and dumb. The bishop was so pleased with his recovery that he offered to give him a permanent place in his household, but the lad preferred to return to his own home.

Francis of Assisi (d. 1226) suffered much ill health himself, due largely to his mode of living in extreme poverty, and he tended to be severe in his attitude towards those of his followers who complained when they were ill. The first version of his rule for the members of his community reads:

> If the sick brother is ill-tempered and complains against God and his brethren, or if he persistently demands medicine in his anxiety to restore his body—which is soon to perish and is an enemy of the soul—he shows himself to be prompted by the flesh and the devil, and he is unworthy to be one of the brethren because he loved his body better than his soul.

That was the first *Rule*, written in 1210. Ten years later it was revised to read: "If any friar falls sick, the others are to look after him as they would wish to be cared for themselves."

Franciscan severity had softened. Perhaps this was partly due to the experience of many healings in those who came to Francis to ask him to pray for them.

Thomas Celano, one of the first biographers of the saint, records a number of miraculous healings. One concerned a small under-developed and paralyzed child in Toscanella:

The boy's father, seeing the man of God to be endued with such holiness, humbly fell at his feet and besought him to heal his son. Francis, deeming himself to be unprofitable and unworthy of such power and grace, for a long time refused to do it. At last, conquered by the urgency of the man's entreaties, after offering up prayer, he laid his hand on the boy, blessed him, and lifted him up. And in the sight of all, the boy straightaway arose whole in the name of our Lord Jesus Christ, and began to walk hither and thither about the house.

The way the story was told might have been influenced by the Gospel narrative, but that certainly doesn't mean it was fictional.

Philip Neri (d. 1595) was a priest in Rome whose personal sanctity made him the trusted confessor and adviser of many, including the popes. The community of priests which he founded later became the Congregation of the Oratory, known as the Oratorians. He exercised a ministry of healing through prayer and the laying on of hands. One example reveals the grim medical treatment practiced at the time:

Lucrezia Grazzi had a cancer in one of her breasts and the physicians had determined to apply a hot iron to it, and ordered her to remain in bed for the operation. She, however, took herself to Philip and related her case to him. He answered, "O, my poor child, where is this cancer?" She pointed to it, saying, "Here, my father." Then the saint, touching the diseased part, added "Go in peace and doubt not that you shall recover." When she was come home, she said to those who were present, "I feel neither pain nor oppression, and I firmly believe I am cured." And so it proved to be. Soon after the physicians came to cauterize the cancer and were lost in astonishment at finding not a trace of the disease.

John Wesley (d. 1791), who published a book called *Primitive Physick* (1747) as a home guide for local preachers, was involved in about two hundred cases of healing through prayer. Many of these are recorded in his diary, such as this one on April 24, 1782:

On Friday I got to Halifax, where Mr. Floyd lay in a high fever, almost dead for want of sleep. This was prevented by the violent

pain in one of his feet, which was much swelled and so sore that it
could not be touched. We joined in prayer that God would fulfil
his word, and give his beloved sleep. Presently the swelling, the
soreness, the pain were gone; and he had a good night's rest.

Pilgrimages have remained an important feature of Christian
discipleship down to our own age. In spite of the superstition and
commercialism associated with them—unfolded in works like
Chaucer's *Canterbury Tales*—they have been a means through which
generations of believers have found God's forgiveness and healing.
Lourdes is the most famous contemporary example; long before the
days of jet travel and ambulances, the sick went or were taken to
places of pilgrimage near their own homes. In England before the
Reformation, hundreds of churches and tombs and holy wells
acquired reputations as places of healing. They kept alive the hope of
a charismatic gift when the only sacramental ministry being offered
was one for the dying.

So, then, our survey shows how the ministry to the sick was
diversified and misinterpreted over the centuries and became
entangled with cultural and social trends. One of the best books I
know on the subject, Morton T. Kelsey's *Healing and Christianity*
(1973), shows how both Catholic and Protestant theology turned
away from expecting God to work miraculously through healings,
deliverances, visions, and charismatic gifts, while different strands of
popular devotion hoped for divine interventions in the highways and
byways of church life. The pastoral care of the sick with sacramental
signs and charismatic power, united in the healing ministry of Jesus
Christ and his apostles, were never completely lost. Like the waters
of a stream, they bubbled out in other channels when their normal
course within the official structures of the church was blocked to
them.

That sets the background for the account of how that ministry is
being restored again within the church now—the subject of the next
chapter.

FIVE

Restoring the Ministry

T HE EXTRAORDINARY GROWTH of medical science from the turn of the century caused many in the church to assume that God's gifts of healing now came through the medical profession, and that the church's ministry to the sick was confined to purely practical and devotional support. Belief in God's direct healing of the sick through sacramental signs and charismatic power was to be found only among smaller Christian groups on the margins of the mainline denominations. The Bible was reinterpreted to accord with contemporary views about the origin of the universe and the history of mankind, and theologies which were labelled liberalism or modernism by their opponents found no place for the miraculous in their teachings.

Yet the hope that God would still heal in response to prayer slowly began to work its way back into those denominations. That hope came from two widely different sources. For convenience we shall call them Catholic and Pentecostal. The Catholic source emerged at the end of the nineteenth century, initially among Anglo-Catholics in the Church of England and in other provinces in the Anglican communion; it eventually affected individuals and groups in the Roman Catholic church, too. The Pentecostal source stemmed from the Holiness revivals which later became the classic Pentecostal churches of our own time.

We will trace these two sources separately.

The Catholic Source

Anglo-Catholics are the spiritual heirs of the Oxford Movement. That movement did much to reassert the claim that the Anglican communion is a branch of the one, holy catholic and apostolic church of the creeds, founded by Jesus Christ and obedient to the Holy Spirit in Scripture and tradition. Anglo-Catholics were concerned, among other things, that Anglicans should enjoy the full sacramental and liturgical life which they regarded as properly belonging to the church—including the sacramental ministry to the sick in anointing and laying on of hands. They took their inspiration from many sources—patristic teachings, medieval liturgical practices, contemporary Roman Catholicism, Eastern Orthodoxy—in varying degrees (though they were sufficiently sensitive to the New Testament not to use the liturgy for the sick as the last rites for the dying to the same extent as their Roman Catholic brethren did). Among these inspirations came a small one from the Catholic Apostolic church.

This body was descended from the congregation which followed Edward Irving after he had been ejected from the Church of Scotland. Irving was a Scottish minister who created much controversy in London in the 1820s and 1830s through his preaching and style of worship. He taught that the charismatic gifts of the New Testament were still available for Christians, including the gift of healing. After his death in 1834 his followers evolved into the Catholic Apostolic church, in which a highly sacramental and ritualistic form of worship was combined with a Pentecostal spirit. Although relatively small, its influence on Anglo-Catholics who encountered it was considerable.

In 1904 F. W. Fuller, a member of the Anglican religious community named the Society of St. John the Evangelist ("the Cowley Fathers"), published a book entitled, *Anointing of the Sick in Scripture and Tradition.* In it he expounded the church's ministry of healing through unction with the laying on of hands, with an exposition of key scripture passages and many examples drawn from Christian history. He pleaded that the Anglican communion was denying the sick the grace covenanted for them in the gospel, and he urged the clergy to embark more boldly on this ministry. The book was important for it demonstrated that the ministry of healing was not a deviation from Christian tradition, as so many assumed, but in the very heart of the Catholic faith.

Eight years later Percy Dearmer, a parish priest in London who was becoming recognized as an expert on liturgy and pastoral care, wrote *Body and Soul*. This was a pioneering volume in which he brought together the church's sacramental ministry to the sick with the charismatic ministry of healing which was being practiced in Holiness-Pentecostal circles, together with what was then the strange new science of analytical psychology. Like the classic Pentecostals, Dearmer stressed that the salvation Christ brings can include physical as well as spiritual healing. He wrote: "A religion that ignores the physical effect of the Spirit—health, that is to say—and the spiritual element in healing, is clearly not commensurate with the Christianity of Christ." He drew on Fuller's material (and added some of his own) to relate what he said to the church's practices in the past. He urged, too, that the church should cooperate more with the medical profession.

The work of Fuller and Dearmer was developed in an essay which Charles Harris, another Anglican priest, contributed to the volume, *Liturgy and Worship,* published in 1932 and designed as a companion to the *Revised Prayer Book* of 1928. Harris used his opportunity to show how inadequate was the Anglican rite for the visitation of the sick when compared with the riches which were available within the church's ancient sacramental teaching. *Liturgy and Worship* was prescribed reading for Anglican theological students round the world since the day it was published, and it was reprinted many times. Any young Anglican priest who wanted to learn more about the church's ministry to the sick when he was called to help them in a parish would automatically have turned to Harris's essay.

Alongside the work of individual Anglican scholars and pastors came the formation of various societies to encourage the ministry of healing. These have proliferated over the years. We will mention three of the earliest as examples.

The Guild of Health was founded in 1904 with Percy Dearmer as its chairman and Conrad Noel, another parish priest well known for his socialist views, as one of its members. Its aim was "to restore the healing ministry of Christ in and through his church" and "to bring together Christian people, particularly doctors, psychiatrists, and ministers of religion to work in fellowship for fuller health, both for the individual and the community."

The following year James Moore Hickson founded the Society of

Emmanuel, later to become the Divine Healing Mission. Hickson was a notable charismatic lay healer. A member of the Church of England, he discovered his gift of healing when at the age of fourteen he felt moved to lay hands on a cousin suffering from neuralgia and she received immediate relief. In 1908 he published a pamphlet, "The Healing of Christ in his Church," which so impressed the Archbishop of Canterbury, Randall Davidson, that he sent a copy to all the Anglican bishops who were assembling for the Lambeth Conference. In 1921 Hickson embarked on a world tour which took him to America, South Africa, Palestine, India, China, Japan, Australia, and New Zealand. His life and ministry is a reminder that even at the beginning of this century charismatic gifts of healing were not confined to Pentecostal circles.

The Guild of Health and the Divine Healing Mission were (and still are) ecumenical membership. The Guild of St. Raphael was founded in 1915 as an exclusively Anglican society to restore the ministry of healing as part of the normal life of the Anglican communion. It was aimed at the high church constituency, as the first of its three objectives shows:

1. To unite in a fellowship of prayer within the Catholic church, those who hold the faith that our Lord wills to work in and through his church for the health of her members in spirit, mind, and body.
2. To promote the belief that God wills the conquest of disease, as well as sin, through the power of the living Christ.
3. To guide the sick and those who care for them to Christ as the source of healing.

The Guild published a good deal of literature, including *St. Raphael's Prayer Book,* which contains a service of prayer for the laying on of hands and anointing of the sick. Practically every Anglican clergyman who has introduced this ministry to the sick in his parish has used this service.

It is through the influence of such societies that some Anglicans moved further into the ministry of healing. Resolutions about the ministry of healing have appeared in the reports of the Lambeth conferences since 1908 (no doubt due to Hickson's paper), and many dioceses and provinces have provided guidelines for those embarking on this ministry.

But Hickson was not the only Anglican to exercise a ministry of healing. Dorothy Kerin and George Bennett were two of a small but growing company who ministered to the sick through prayer, the laying on of hands, and anointing in the period before and after World War II.

Dorothy Kerin (1889-1963) was miraculously healed when she was near death with advanced tuberculosis and diabetes at the age of twenty-two. After her healing she had a series of mystical experiences of union with the suffering of mankind, including the troops at the front in World War I; it is said that during the course of these experiences she received the stigmata. After the war she opened a house of healing in the Culmington Road, Ealing. This was followed by other ventures until eventually Burrswood near Tunbridge Wells was purchased in 1948. To this large house came the sick, some to stay for a few days, many to receive prayer with the laying on of hands, from Dorothy and her community. Healing services were held in the Church of Christ the Healer, built on the grounds. In the 1950s I attended one of these and watched Dorothy in her white robe moving along the communion rail and praying with people who were kneeling there.

She wrote:

> We have come to know that with God—our living God—nothing is impossible, and for those who have eyes to see and ears to hear the message is still true—"I am the Lord that healeth thee." His arm is not shortened, his power is not less than in those days two thousand years ago when he walked among us healing all who came to him.

George Bennett (1910-78) trained as a medical student. Later in life he was ordained an Anglican priest, and his healing ministry developed out of his experience as a hospital chaplain, as a canon of Coventry Cathedral, and as warden of the Divine Healing Mission's headquarters at Crowhurst in East Sussex. From 1969 until his death he traveled extensively to teach and practice the ministry of healing. "I often feel," he used to say, "that what we have in the gospel is not so much a ministry of healing but rather a glorious gospel which is so tremendous that it meets all the needs of man at every point. No one is left out."

Although I have written only of Anglican societies and individuals in the movement to restore the ministry of healing to the church (and among those outside Pentecostal circles, Anglicans seem to have taken most of the initiatives), members in other denominations were becoming more interested, too. Not everyone was swept along by the dispensationalism which was current in evangelical and most other theological circles. A revived understanding of the church as the body of Christ, and a greater appreciation of sacramental signs as means of God's grace, focused attention on prayer with the laying on of hands and anointing. In dismissing the Roman Catholic practice as unscriptural, Protestants asked what was the true biblical use of these gifts. So groups like the Methodist Sacramental Fellowship encouraged members to use the anointing and laying on of hands with the sick for healing.

In the meantime changes were slowly taking place in the Roman Catholic church itself. As we have seen, the Council of Trent did not completely endorse the medieval view that anointing and the laying on of hands was a rite only for the dying, and pastoral practice varied in different parts of the world. With the revival of biblical and liturgical scholarship some Roman Catholics began to realize the discrepancy between what the New Testament taught and what was practiced in parishes, and several papal statements in the years before the Second Vatican Council suggested that it was not only those who were in danger of death who should be anointed but those who were seriously ill. By the time of the Second Vatican Council there was a build-up of scholarly and pastoral opinion that unction should be restored as a sacrament for healing. This was tentatively acknowledged by the Council:

> "Extreme unction," which may be more fittingly called "anointing of the sick," is not a sacrament for those only who are at the point of death. Hence, as soon as any of the faithful begins to be in danger of death from sickness or old age, the appropriate time for him to receive this sacrament has already arrived.

It was not much, but it was the opening the liturgists wanted.

Their revision of the liturgy for the sick went far beyond what was envisaged by the Council. When published in 1974, it contained forms of use in different situations. It can still be used as "extreme unction," but it has prayers for use with those suffering from less serious illnesses. In the instructions which accompany it, priests are directed to use it for any of the sick who are under their pastoral care, including the aged and infirm and those about to undergo surgery. They should not just anoint them but counsel them, read the Scriptures with them, bring them communion, and hear their confession if they desire it.

The instructions remind the laity that they, too, have a ministry to the sick, praying with them and giving them support and encouragement and practical care. Relatives and friends as well as doctors and nurses are invited to take part in the sacramental ministry, and there is a form of blessing of the oil for use by the laity.

But forms of services and revivals of sacraments cannot in themselves restore the ministry of healing to the church. They may provide Bible readings and prayers, scriptural signs and comforting gestures; but it is what those who minister to the sick and what the sick themselves hope for that matters. Sacramental ministrations do not operate in a vacuum. With them there must be a renewal of faith in the power of the Holy Spirit.

Such a spiritual renewal has come from the classic Pentecostal churches. Its influence was later than the Catholic source; but when the two began to run together, the church's ministry of healing began to be restored to its pastoral, sacramental, and charismatic wholeness.

The Pentecostal Source

The claim that spiritual gifts of healing could still be experienced in the church was made chiefly—although not exclusively—in the Holiness groups which evolved alongside the evangelical churches in the latter half of the nineteenth century. These groups originated in the religious revivals of North America which spread to Europe and other parts of the world; they were distinctive in Protestant Christianity because they taught that through the Holy Spirit believers can be made holy in their personal lives. Because they are filled with or baptized in the Holy Spirit, believers are sanctified and experience victory over Satan through the power of God. (The more extreme view was that sanctification should be so complete that the Christian should expect to live in perfect obedience to God. Also, he should expect to live in perfect health!)

With such an understanding of God's power, and with such a literalist view of the Bible, it was logical that Holiness congregations should believe in physical healing. The healing ministry, with ministries of deliverance from evil spirits, was therefore part of their stock in trade. Some of them even took the text, "They will pick up serpents" (Mark 16:18), at its face value and incorporated this dangerous practice into their worship, as do the Snakehandlers of West Virginia today.

To illustrate the effect of the healing ministry of the Holiness churches, I will describe briefly the lives of two of their most outstanding leaders. Both were of Scottish descent—Andrew Murray (1828-1917) and John Alexander Dowie (1847-1905).

Andrew Murray was born in South Africa, the son of a Dutch Reformed minister. With his brother, John, he was sent to Aberdeen and then to Utrecht to study theology, and he returned to South Africa as a minister in the Dutch Reformed church. His last pastorate was in Wellington, where he remained for forty-five years. He was deeply influenced by Holiness teachings, experienced a baptism in the Holy Spirit, and taught that healing came through prayer for those who were saved by the power of the Spirit.

> Sick Christian, open thy Bible, study it and see in its pages that sickness is a warning to renounce sin, but that whoever acknowledges and forsakes his sins finds in Jesus pardon and healing. Such is God's promise in his Word. If the Lord had in view some other dispensation for such of his children whom he was about to call home to him, he would make known to them his will, giving them by the Holy Spirit a desire to depart; in other special cases, he would awaken some special conviction; but, as a general rule, the Word of God promises us healing in answer to the prayer of faith. . . . "This is the will of God, even your sanctification" (1 Thess 4:3), and it is by healing that God confirms the reality of this. When Jesus comes to take possession of our body, and cures miraculously, when it follows that health received must be maintained from day to day by an uninterrupted

communion with him, the experience which we thus make of the Saviour's power and of his love is a result very superior to any which sickness has to offer.

Through his world tours and through his books, which are still reprinted, Murray has exercised a wide influence in promoting the ministry of healing through charismatic gifts.

John Alexander Dowie was born in Edinburgh. He was sent to live with his uncle in Australia when he was thirteen, but returned to Edinburgh as a student of theology a few years later. In Edinburgh he acted as an unofficial hospital chaplain; his conversations with surgeons may have caused his aversion to the medical profession which persisted for the rest of his life. He became a Congregational minister in Australia and rapidly acquired a reputation as a revivalist preacher. He moved to the United States in 1888 to minister in the Zion Tabernacle in Chicago, where the healing of a cousin of Abraham Lincoln through his ministry gave him enormous publicity.

He had a vision of a city created without institutional links to sinful practices—no liquor stores, theatres, doctors, or hospitals! He set out to create such a city in Zion, Illinois, and built a vast temple for twenty-five thousand people and set up a lace industry run on a cooperative basis. He embarked on evangelistic tours in North America and in other parts of the world, and the ministry of healing was always to the forefront of his program.

Dowie set out his teaching in eight points:

> God's way of healing is a person, not a thing. The Lord Jesus Christ is still the healer. Divine healing rests on Christ's atonement. Disease can never be God's will. The gifts of healing are permanent. Divine healing is opposed by diabolical counterfeits (Christian Science, mind healing, and so on). Multitudes have been healed through faith in Jesus Christ. Belief cometh of hearing, and hearing by the way of God.

Dowie's commercial enterprises collapsed and towards the end of his life he seems to have suffered from some mental disorder; but many of his followers became the leading Pentecostal preachers at the beginning of the twentieth century in the United States, Europe, and South Africa. It was some of these followers who established the Christian Catholic Church of Zion in South Africa, which later developed into the Pentecostal Apostolic Faith Mission, with its great stress on the ministry of healing. This Mission was one of the roots of the present day black independent churches in the African continent. Walter Hollenweger, in *The Pentecostals* (1972), wrote that Dowie did more than any other evangelist to bring the ministry of healing into the foreground of Christian consciousness in this century.

The classic Pentecostal churches emerged out of this Holiness tradition with their powerful stress on the spiritual gifts of healing. Charles Parham, who founded the Bethel Bible School in Topeka where students were involved in a Pentecostal experience of speaking in tongues, was a faith healer prior to that incident in 1901. One of his students at another Bible school in Houston, Texas, was W.J. Seymour, who was at the center of the Azusa Street revival and who is regarded as the first Pentecostal minister. The accepted view among the Pentecostal churches was that when a Christian turned to the Spirit-filled community for healing, he should expect God to cure him without medical aid. No revival meeting was considered a success unless several healings took place.

In the early years of the Pentecostal churches it was regarded as sinful to take medicine or to go to a doctor if you had been ministered to for healing. One American preacher, F.M. Britton, refused medical aid for his son and reported later that the lad had died "without drugs." Some years later his wife also died after refusing medicine. Although threatened with jail for refusing to let his family receive medical attention, Britton never wavered in his views. In 1915 another Pentecostal preacher, Walter Barney, a Church of God minister from Wytheville, Virginia, was convicted of manslaughter for refusing to let a doctor see his daughter, who later died, but his conviction was overturned by the governor of Virginia. Such cases were not exceptional.

Soon, however, the question of whether or not to accept medical aid became one of the factors in causing divisions. In 1920 the Pentecostal Holiness church split over the issue, and the group which held that medical care should go along with the ministry of healing became the Congregational Holiness church which spread over the states of Georgia, Alabama, Florida, North Carolina, and

South Carolina. Nowadays it is no longer an issue. Most Pentecostals see medical care as in partnership with the healing ministry of
their churches.

We ought to note two other characteristics of the classic
Pentecostal healing ministry which later left their mark on the new
Pentecostal movement. The first is that in both the Holiness and the
Pentecostal traditions there is usually an open recognition of the
ministry of women, even among those churches which will not allow
a woman to lead a congregation. They read in Joel 2:28, "Your sons
and your daughters shall prophesy," and they therefore welcomed
those women who exercised spiritual gifts for the building up of the
people of God, especially gifts of healing.

One of the first women preachers to gain fame in the United States
as a faith healer was Mary Woodworth Etter, whose divine healing
campaigns in the 1890s led her through Florida, South Carolina,
Indiana, Iowa, and Missouri. In sensational meetings in churches,
tents, and auditoriums, Mrs. Etter claimed to have cured people of
cancer, dumbness, tumors, deafness, and so on. Not even Aimee
Semple McPherson, a generation later, could match such claims.
Women have also been leaders in this ministry among the new
Pentecostals—Kathryn Kuhlman, Agnes Sanford, Barbara Leahy
Shlemon, Ann Thérèse Shields. Problems about whether or not
women can be ministers shrivel to insignificance when through their
prayers sick people are healed!

The second characteristic of the classic Pentecostal healing
ministry we ought to note is the use of the charism known as "a word
of knowledge." This spiritual gift, from the list in 1 Corinthians 12,
is accepted by Pentecostals as a means whereby the Holy Spirit
reveals to the one who ministers insight into the needs and personal
circumstances of those to whom he ministers—insights which would
not be available through the normal means of communication. So,
for example, a Pentecostal preacher will end his sermon with a time
of open prayer during which he will receive "words from the Lord"
telling him about various people in the congregation: "The Lord is
telling me that there's a lady here with a twisted spine—she's had it
since she was twelve years old, when she fell downstairs. The Lord is
healing her right now. She's to receive his healing by faith. . . . And
there's a man who has to go to the hospital next week with suspected
heart trouble. The Lord's healing him, too. When he goes for his

examination next week, the doctors will find nothing. . . ." This style of ministry has also been adopted by some new Pentecostals.

The ministry of healing, then, is deeply rooted in the Pentecostal tradition. In the Declaration of Faith of the Elim Pentecostal churches it is laid down "we believe that our Lord Jesus Christ is the healer of the body, and that all who walk in obedience to him will claim divine healing for their bodies." The Assemblies of God are just as specific: "Deliverance from sickness is provided for in the atonement, and is the privilege of all believers (Is 53:4-5; Mt 8:16-17)."

Oral Roberts is one of the best-known leaders in the ministry of healing today. He asks for cases of healing by prayer to be medically tested, and he publishes only accounts of cases of healing where the recovery has been maintained for a long period under medical supervision. The university which he founded in Tulsa, Oklahoma, has a faculty of medicine equipped with modern means of research.

The New Pentecostal Synthesis

On the face of it, no two Christian traditions could seem further apart than the Catholicism of the Roman and Anglican communions and the Pentecostalism which sprang from Holiness and fundamentalist congregations. In terms of worship and church structure they could hardly be more different. Yet in spite of this, both traditions are united in an expectant belief that God is one who still speaks and acts among his people in this world. They stand together on this faith over against the questioning of the liberal-modernist traditions, who sometimes give the impression that if God is not dead, then he is imprisoned by the ideas and impulses of the humanity he has created. To put it simply—Catholics and Pentecostals believe in miracles. And that makes a lot of difference in one's approach to the ministry of healing!

There is also another basic similarity. Both Pentecostal Christianity and Catholic Christianity are profoundly sacramental. Pentecostals do not theologize about their beliefs and practices as Catholics do: it is enough for them that what they do and say reflects the teaching of the Bible, as they understand it. With this goes a sense of the goodness of the things God has created—even if those things are spoiled by evil in various forms. So the Pentecostal is prepared to express himself using his body as a means of worship—clapping his hands, swaying his hips, lifting his arms in the air, embracing his neighbor. And he is prepared to use in worship the things that are used in the New Testament as instruments of Christ's presence and the Spirit's power—water, bread, wine, oil, the laying on of hands.

All this represents a meeting point with Catholic sacramentalism in spite of the differences in theology and practice. Both share a common *experience* of God's grace in Jesus Christ through the Holy Spirit, even if the theological understanding and cultural setting of that experience are varied. What was needed to bring them together was an acceptance of one another as recipients of the varying gifts of the one Spirit in the body of Christ.

That synthesis is being achieved in this ecumenical age through many contacts in local councils of churches, conferences, joint ministries, common challenges, and opportunities in an increasingly secular and multi-faith society. Women and men of God recognize and respect one another when they meet, in spite of their different backgrounds. The Holy Spirit is a uniting power, breaking down even theological and cultural barriers when he sets the disciples of Christ on fire with God's love.

In the last twenty years or so, it has been the new Pentecostal movement which has done more than any other spiritual renewal among Christians to effect this synthesis. Greater faith in the gifts of the Spirit has resulted in greater unity among women and men who are open to the Spirit; and as the ministry of healing has spread with the new Pentecostal movement among the denominations across the world, so Christians everywhere have found themselves drawing on Catholic and Pentecostal resources and finding in them the riches of the gospel.

That, then, is the story of the church's ministry of healing up to the present day and a brief explanation of why it is being restored in the midst of contemporary spiritual renewal. In the second half of this book I want to discuss different aspects of this healing ministry and suggest ways in which we can follow the Holy Spirit in our churches as he reveals, through healing, signs of God's kingdom to our sick and dying world.

Part Two

SIX

Forgiveness and Freedom

Forgiveness of sins and renewal in the Holy Spirit is the foundation for true healing. At the center of the gospel is the revelation of the mystery of which Isaiah prophesied, "With his stripes we are healed" (Is 53:5), and the church's ministry is to help its members reach for and grasp the reality of this mystery in their own lives. In the Messiah, the Spirit-anointed One, God offers a balm to sin-sick humanity. To repent, to turn to Christ and to receive the Holy Spirit is how we accept that offer and continue our pilgrimage to his kingdom, our salvation.

Confession of our sins, then, is the first step in seeking a gift of healing for physical, mental, and emotional ills. Although Jesus Christ refuted the Old Testament concept of sickness as a punishment for personal sin, his teaching and that of the rest of the New Testament leave us in no doubt that sickness and sinfulness are intertwined in a deadly fashion. None of us is free from the corporate effects of human sinfulness, even if our individual weaknesses are not a direct factor in our suffering. The exploitation of individuals and peoples through greed, jealousy, ambition, lust, pride; injuries and disfigurements that result from terrorism and warfare (and the long-distant causes of those evils); the scars on an individual's thoughts and feelings brought about by ill treatment and unloving behavior; the damage to our environment through unthinking industrial and scientific development—these things cannot be quantified, but it so often seems that much of the suffering we humans experience on this planet is brought about through our own wickedness.

Then there is the sickness in society itself which infests its own members. This is vividly reflected in what is presented for so-called entertainment on radio and television, on screen and stage. The media is a kind of mirror of ourselves. Through it we recognize our increasing permissiveness and assumptions about violence, greed, ambition, and sexual misbehavior.

Added to this is widespread confusion, within the church as well as outside it, about the nature of sin itself. Reasonable-sounding questions are asked. Can we really be blamed for revolting against authority when our age has seen such gross abuses of authority? Are we really culpable for hating our neighbor when we have not experienced love ourselves in our formative years? Determinism like this ultimately takes away responsibility for our actions. We become human computers working to a prearranged psychological program in one situation after another. It implies we have no choice. Sin becomes a myth.

But that is not what God has said. The story of salvation unfolded in the Bible underlines the fundamental truth that we are created with a moral sense, even if our consciences need further enlightenment through the law of God and the experience of his love in Jesus Christ. Whatever reasons there may be for a diminished sense of responsibility—and we shall discuss some aspects of that in the next chapter—the gospel announces our healing, our salvation, begins when we repent of our sins. The confession and forgiveness of sins is our primary spiritual therapy.

For this reason baptism is, among other things, a sacrament of healing. When we are baptized we are immersed in the liberating death of Christ where our sins are buried, where the "old Adam" in us is crucified with Christ, and where the power of sin within us is broken. We are raised to a new life in the power of the resurrection, knowing that through the Holy Spirit we will ultimately be one with Christ in a resurrection like his (Rom 6:3-11; Col 2:13, 3:1; Eph 2:5-6).

Occasionally the spiritual rebirth of baptism is accompanied by outward and visible healing. One man I prepared for baptism and confirmation completely lost an embarrassing stutter after he had been initiated into the church. A woman I presented for con-firmation discovered after the service that she had been freed from an addiction to smoking. Neither I nor the candidates had expected these cures. They were added bonuses from God to the repentance, faith, and gift of the Holy Spirit which the sacramental signs offered.

But although baptism initiates us into the new life of Christ, we are not shielded from temptations. We are still liable to fall into sin and become separate from God through our disobedience. That is why the ministry of healing begins with a renewal of repentance and faith and a fresh openness to the Spirit of God. Those who seek God's healing grace must ensure that nothing on their side acts as a barrier.

The way in which we seek God's mercy and forgiveness will obviously vary in different circumstances. What is essential is that we tell God we are sorry for our sins, promise we will amend our lives in his strength, and ask for his forgiveness. It is a necessary precon-dition that we should be willing to ask for the forgiveness of those we have wronged and also be willing to forgive those who have wronged us.

The Lord's Prayer puts this intention on our lips: "Forgive us our debts, as we also have forgiven our debtors" (Mt 6:12; Lk 11:4). Most church services include prayers of forgiveness and absolution in which we are invited to join. But at certain times, and particularly at moments of personal crisis like the onset of a serious illness, we may need help in making our confession and in receiving forgiveness from God through the ministry of the church.

A Ministry of Reconciliation

The church believes that, under the anointing of the Holy Spirit, she is authorized by Jesus Christ to pronounce the absolution of sins to those who confess them (Mt 18:18; Jn 20:23; Jas 5:16). Obviously there can be nothing automatic about this. The mere formality of making our confession does not qualify us to receive God's pardon. But where a Christian in genuine repentance asks another to pray for the Lord's forgiveness for specific faults, there is scriptural assurance that God hears that prayer.

In ecclesiastical jargon this practice has been known traditionally as "going to confession." It is not the happiest title. For one thing, it tends to be associated in non-Catholic minds with the Reformation protest against the abuse of priestly authority. For another, the actual confession of faults is but a preliminary to the real blessing the discipline brings, the assurance of forgiveness which God gives us through his Son. The "ministry of reconciliation" is a better title and one that is employed more often nowadays.

The ministry of reconciliation brings us healing in two ways: it brings us the personal healing which comes when we are at peace with God, and it brings corporate healing within the body of Christ.

This corporate healing is often overlooked, yet it is a consequence of our being members one of another in the body of Christ. My sins are like a cancer in the church. Even my most intimate faults, known perhaps only to myself, are weaknesses within the fellowship because they breach the relationship I have in Christ with God. If I sin against God, then I also sin against God's people. This is the implication of what Paul meant when he said, "If one member suffers, all suffer together" (1 Cor 12:26). Our sins are the dark opposite of our spiritual gifts: charisms build up the body of Christ and glorify the Lord, whereas sins deny Christ and weaken his church. The presence of an unrepentant sinner in the Corinthian congregation prompted the apostle to order his expulsion, for his presence contaminated the holiness of the community (1 Cor 5).

The manner in which this ministry of reconciliation has been exercised has varied enormously. In the early centuries it evolved as an act of worship which demonstrated that forgiveness included reconciliation with the church as well as with God. The sinner confessed his faults privately to his bishop or presbyter, but was then enrolled in what was known as "the order of penitents." He was allowed to come to church, but he had to stand at the back and refrain from receiving communion. The congregation (who might or might not know what his fault was) said prayers for him and he undertook fasts and other penitential exercises to demonstrate the genuineness of his sorrow.

He usually remained a penitent for some time—the season of Lent was the formal period for this. When Easter approached, he was absolved and reconciled through prayers offered by the bishop at a service during Holy Week. The bishop laid his hands on the penitent's head as a sign that the offender was forgiven and was receiving the Holy Spirit afresh. Then he joined with the rest of the congregation in sharing in the eucharist on Easter morning. The symbolism of this was powerful indeed. His reconciliation had taken place within the fellowship of God's people. He had died once more to his sins and risen again in Christ through repentance. He rejoiced with God's other daughters and sons in celebrating the resurrection. Christian teachers referred to it as "the second baptism" (a fact which might be relevant when pastors are asked for a second baptism these days).

One of the most famous preachers of the early church, John Chrysostom (John the golden-mouthed), used the analogy of healing when he urged his congregation in Antioch to undertake this discipline one Lent:

> Confess your sins in order that you may be saved. Why, I ask, are you ashamed to tell your sins? Do you tell them to a man, so that he may shame you? Of course not! It is to the Lord that you show your wounds. He is the physician who cares for you. And the Lord says to you, "Tell me your sins that I may heal your wounds and relieve your pain."

This form of public penance gradually dropped out of use. It became too onerous for many Christians, and there were obvious disadvantages in being made a spectacle before a congregation. Confessions were made and absolutions given privately. Yet, for all its weaknesses, the older form did reveal one scriptural truth about forgiveness: our sins are offences against God's people as well as against God, and that when we are forgiven we should be forgiven on earth as well as in heaven.

Confession of one's sins to another Christian seems to have been practiced throughout the church's history. The highly stylized form of the Roman Catholic confessional is only one method of exercising this discipline; it has been done more informally in different ways when a church member has gone to the pastor for a confidential talk. One effect of telling another our faults is to make us feel ashamed for them. Saying we are sorry (and meaning it) is not always easy. We assume that God knows our faults anyway and therefore to confess them is to tell him what he already knows. Confessing them to God before another is quite a different matter!

Another advantage is that the Lord often endows with gifts of wisdom those who hear our confessions. They see things to which we are blind, and they are inspired to give us God's word in our predicament. The Roman Catholic service instructs the priest to pray for God's assistance before he hears confessions, especially for discernment: "The discernment of spirits consists of a deep knowledge of the works of God in the human heart, and is a gift of the Holy Spirit and one of the fruits of love."

It was the prospect of receiving counsel from the holy and the wise that led to the custom in eastern Christianity of confessing sins not only to priests but to spiritually mature lay men and women as well. The monks were sought out for this purpose. The custom goes back to the days of Antony, a man of prayer who sought God in the solitude of the African desert at about the same time as John Chrysostom was preaching in Antioch. Antony is regarded as the father of monasticism, and he was so much sought after as a confessor that he became known as "the physician of all Egypt."

In Russia such confessors were known as "elders" (*staretz*, plural, *startsi*). One of the greatest of the *startsi* was Seraphim of Sarov (d. 1833). After fifteen years as a monk, he withdrew into a hut in the Russian forests and lived in seclusion for thirty years. Then in 1825 he opened the door of his hut to visitors, and for the remainder of his life thousands came to seek his ministry.

A man called Motovilov called one day and was dazzled by the light which was shining so brightly in the monk's face that the visitor was unable to look at him.

"Don't be afraid," said Seraphim. "At this very moment you have become as bright as I am. You yourself are now in the fullness of God's Spirit."

He laid his hands on Motovilov's shoulder.

"How do you feel?"

"An immeasurable healing," said the visitor. "I feel such a calm, such a peace in my soul that no words can express it."

"That is the peace which the risen Lord gave to his disciples," said the monk. "And what else do you feel?"

"I feel an infinite joy as well."

"When the Spirit of God comes down on a man and overshadows him," the monk went on, "then that man's soul overflows with unspeakable joy, for the Holy Spirit fills with joy whoever he touches."

To say that we are healed when we repent of our sins and receive the forgiveness of God, then, is not just to employ a vivid analogy of what happens. It describes the spiritual and psychological healing which accompanies the open confession of our faults before another sister or brother in the Lord. Most of us at one time or another have experienced the enormous relief which comes after we have owned up to some misdemeanor. The ministry of reconciliation expresses this in a sacramental manner. Through the prayers offered by those who hear our confession we are touched by the cleansing blood of Christ and reunited with him in his church.

I was involved recently in making a video for teaching purposes on the sacramental liturgy of the church. We wanted to include some clips of a penitent making his confession to a priest, so we asked a Roman Catholic priest to arrange a mock-up of this ministry with one of his congregation. We took the camera, recording equipment, and lighting into his church, and filmed the priest and his parishioner as they sat together in a quiet corner of a side chapel. After saying aloud the formal part of the liturgy (we faded out the microphone at the point where the penitent was supposed to be declaring his sins!), the TV screen showed the priest and the penitent chatting together in an easy, friendly fashion. At the end of their conversation, the priest stood up and laid his hands on the penitent's head as he said the prayer of absolution. It struck me, as I watched, that the scene could also have been used to illustrate the ministry of healing.

This impression was strengthened after the penitent had thanked the priest and returned to his place in a pew. We heard him say aloud one of the prayers of thanksgiving provided in the Roman rite for this:

> Lord God, you have helped us to overcome our weaknesses. May our lives bear witness to the saving power that has healed us, and may we rejoice in it always, through Jesus Christ our Lord.

That, too, would have been appropriate after receiving ministry for healing.

Of course, a good deal of mutual forgiveness and reconciliation takes place informally when members of a congregation meet each other and do things together. No Christian who is learning to walk in the Spirit can allow a situation to develop where he or she breaks off relationships with another. That is not only spiritually weakening; bitterness between individuals in a family or among friends can cause ill health. The promptings of the Spirit will nudge us towards reconciliation.

Small groups in church fellowships are sometimes places where a form of confession takes place—especially where an individual is seeking to be delivered from a personal fault. This development needs careful pastoral supervision. The history of confessions in groups is not a happy one—in this century the practice among Buchmanites brought the movement into disrepute. The traditional form of confession privately to a priest emerged because on the whole it has seemed the most satisfactory way of exercising this ministry of spiritual healing. Counseling in confidence from a mature Christian can be more appropriate in certain cases. But much depends on the trust established and maintained between the two or three individuals concerned. Once that trust is abused, the ministry breaks down, and the hope of healing is replaced by the experience of pain.

A Ministry of Deliverance

Most Christians experience afresh the freedom of the children of God when they have repented and received from God the forgiveness of their sins. But for a few others this freedom does not come after they have made their confession. They still seem to be trapped in an evil habit or rebellious attitude which refuses to let them go. For the majority of these there are deep psychological problems which may require inner healing, and we shall look at this need in the next chapter. For a small minority a ministry of deliverance is necessary.

I have only been involved in this ministry about ten or a dozen times, so my first-hand experience is limited. But I shall always remember the first occasion which took place when a man came to see me about a personal problem.

He was a likable character, a scientist in an atomic research establishment. He told me the story of his life—his upbringing, his college days when he had been converted to faith in Jesus Christ, his research fellowships in England and in Europe, his marriage, his children, and his church. What bothered him, he said, was that although he understood perfectly well what it meant to love—God, his wife, his family—he could never convince himself that he had actually experienced loving and being loved in return.

He summed it up like this: "It's as if there's a great block of ice where my heart should be. Although I talk about loving and respond to being loved, it all seems so unreal because there's a coldness inside me where I'm sure there would be a warmth."

I questioned him about his childhood and upbringing, discussed his relationships, and made a few guesses. But nothing seemed to reveal the root of his problem. In the end I gave up and suggested we finish the interview with a prayer.

I sat beside him and said one or two prayers before I had an impulse to stand in front of him and lay my hands on his head. I remained like that for a few moments, not knowing what to say. Then I prayed aloud in tongues.

To my alarm he began to shake violently and snort like a horse through his mouth and nose. I held him for a few moments, still praying in tongues.

Suddenly he let out a piercing scream.

"Don't let him come near me!" he shouted. "Keep him away from me."

He pointed fearfully with his left hand over to my right.

I glanced round. There was no one there.

Left hand. An old saying flashed into my mind: "God to the right, the devil to the left."

With an authority which surprised me, I commanded the devil to leave God's servant alone and to trouble him no further. I invoked the name of Jesus Christ and claimed the protection of his cross.

The effect was dramatic. Within a few moments the man was calm again. He stood up and embraced me, his face shining with joy.

"It's gone!" he cried, putting a hand on his heart. "The coldness has gone! I know it has!"

He left with many expressions of gratitude.

A few weeks later he came to see me again, bringing his wife with him.

"My husband's changed," she said; "he loves me in such a wonderfully different way."

"I feel I can love with my heart and the whole of myself—not just with my mind," he told me.

He was like a man who had been released from a long sentence in prison.

"Deliver us from evil," we ask in the Lord's Prayer. The relevance of that petition came to life in a new way for me after that incident.

The new Pentecostals in the denominations have rediscovered the need for this ministry. They see evil as an objective force permeating life to such an extent that certain invalids have to be freed from its power in the authority of Christ's name. Other Christians, however, reject this, saying that belief in Satan belongs to the superstitions of the past and that manifestations of evil—irrational behavior, strange voices, vomiting—can be explained psychologically as examples of hysteric dissociation. The tension caused by this division can be frustrating, especially when someone needs a deliverance ministry and their pastor rejects its validity. The situation is not made any easier by the activities of that minority who see demons everywhere and assume that all healings need deliverance.

Outside new Pentecostal circles, however, attitudes in the denominations are changing. With the rise of interest in the occult and magic, medical practitioners, welfare officers, and even the police are beginning to turn to pastors in the churches known to be experienced in this mysterious and dangerous area. Countless cases make it impossible to ignore the restoration of exorcism in the church's armory in the spiritual battle of our times. It is no longer possible to explain away stories simply in terms of scientific and psychological medicine.

As I have already said, I was doubtful at one time about the reality of satanic influence—as I was about miraculous healing—but, like many other Christians caught up into the new Pentecostal movement, I was forced to re-think my attitudes through what I heard and observed.

I once attended a rally which was addressed by a well-known Christian leader. While he was speaking, a young man in the audience leapt up and screamed abuse at him, gesticulating in a wild and obscene manner. I immediately concluded the man was demented, and went forw. .rd with some ushers who dragged the young man from the hall. Four or five of them carried him down a corridor, restraining him with difficulty, until they got to a room and laid him on the floor.

There was a terrible stench in the atmosphere, not a human smell that I recognized. The ushers evidently knew what they were about, for they invoked the name of Jesus Christ to deliver the young man from the devil. More prayers were offered, and in a few minutes the young man quieted down. Then he sat up, his face transfigured with joy, and asked for a drink of water. He had no recollection of what had happened to him from the time the rally began. As I watched, a phrase from Mark's Gospel seemed apt: "And they came to Jesus, and saw the demoniac sitting there, clothed, and in his right mind" (Mk 5:15).

But I was still a bit anxious.

"Shouldn't we take him to see a doctor?" I asked one of the men who had been exercising the ministry of deliverance for him.

The man I addressed looked at me sharply. "I am a doctor," he said.

The boundary between psychological disorder and spiritual attack is extremely misty. Where does schizophrenia merge with demonic troubling? There are unknown dangers awaiting those who try to enter into this ministry unprepared and inexperienced, without the preparation and support which is so necessary. If you embark on a deliverance ministry by yourself, you are liable to end up in peril, perhaps endangering other people as well.

Satan's most cunning weapon is deceit—giving the appearance of good when in reality it is evil. A trap that some involved in this ministry fall into is the assumption that they alone have a special gift from the Lord to drag poor souls from the devil's grasp. Often their engagement in the ministry of deliverance acts as a cover to their own personal problems, and they find that it gives them a status among their fellow Christians which they did not have before. They see every illness as demonic and they refuse to accept any authority from the church over their ministry. With their small band of admirers, they can wreak havoc. It is noticeable how many of the horror stories about deliverance ministries that went wrong come from small groups of Christians acting in isolation from a wider ecclesiastical oversight.

Most churches now have guidelines about this ministry that usually include the following points:

1. The ministry of deliverance should always be undertaken in a group, preferably in a church building. (Obviously there will be occasions when the need for prayer for deliverance becomes evident when you happen to be alone with the troubled person, as I was in the first case I have just described; but these occasions should be regarded as exceptional.)

2. The group who minister should be accountable to their ecclesiastical authorities (the leaders of the church, congregation, parish, diocese, district, state, or whatever).

3. The group should, if possible, include some who have had previous experience of this ministry.

4. Preliminary counseling should be given and medical advice sought.

5. The spiritual preparation of the client should be carefully monitored.

6. Those who undertake this ministry should prepare with prayer and fasting.

7. The ministry should not be allowed to go on too long. Half-night sessions are not necessary; if nothing happens within an hour, the ministry should be postponed until a further occasion.

8. After the ministry, the client should be incorporated into the Christian fellowship and given aftercare until it is clear he or she is completely free from whatever troubled them.

Guidelines such as these are valuable protection. Troubled individuals have a devilish knack of cornering you at inconvenient moments and making you feel that you're letting them down if you don't do something there and then. How often clergy have told me they were trapped on a case late on a Saturday night, only to find themselves tired and irritable when they got up to lead the worship in their churches on the Sunday morning! The advice of the experienced is: Don't let yourself be manipulated. Be firm that you cannot act until you have sought the help of the pastoral leadership in your congregation. It's good strategy in spiritual warfare (as in physical warfare) to fight the enemy at a time and a place that *you* choose.

A wise Pentecostal pastor once said to me: "Don't go looking for the devil in others; but when he makes himself known, tread on him in the name of the Lord!"

The Power of Forgiveness

The spiritual power of forgiveness and reconciliation is often overlooked by Christians. We tend to think of spiritual power in terms of charisms to fulfill a task in the Lord's name, not in terms of removing obstacles and delivering from evil.

But once a sinner takes the first step towards repentance, he can find himself caught up by the Holy Spirit and carried through to reconciliation by God in Jesus Christ and with those nearest to him in remarkable ways. It is as if the decision to repent removes a log jam in his life, enabling the current of God's love to flow so much more freely. Further difficulties can remain, but they are nothing like the initial difficulty of reaching a decision to seek forgiveness.

A pastor friend of mine was approached one evening by a man who requested an interview with him. The man explained that he was a compulsive gambler and that he had spent all his savings. His wife had ordered him out of the house. In his depressed state, he had contemplated suicide, but had come to see my friend in the vague hope that he might help him.

My friend gave him a meal, talked with him for a long time, and then laid hands on the man's head, praying that he might be released from his compulsion by the power of the Holy Spirit. He made the sign of the cross on the man's forehead before he left.

The man returned about a week later with his wife. She confirmed that her husband was a changed man and that he showed every sign of renouncing forever his compulsion to gamble.

The man then explained to my friend what had happened after he had been to see him. He had gone from the rectory to the only place he knew he would not be disturbed for the night—the lounge of the nearby airport—and, while sitting there for several hours, had had a series of visions. One was of the devil: he didn't go into details, but the vision had been very vivid to him. Another vision had been of a roulette table without any numbers on it. Yet another was of a Roman soldier holding what looked like a bow in his hands.

He believed that the visions had much to do with the change in his life. The first vision had convinced him of the reality of evil and of his urgent need to renounce the desire to gamble. The second had enabled him to see for the first time the utter futility of gambling. In the third he had seen the Roman soldier shaking his head, indicating a firm "No" to gambling because of the broken relationships the habit had caused.

"I can understand the first two visions," he said to my friend, "but I couldn't understand why the third had to be a Roman soldier. As far as I know, I've never had any interest in the Roman army. And why a bow in his hand?"

My friend smiled.

"Do you know the name of this church?"

The man shook his head.

"St. Martin's. He was a Roman soldier, an officer, who left the army when he became a Christian to become an evangelist. Our church is dedicated in his honor. Come and see a picture."

They went into the church. My friend led them into the sanctuary and pointed to a picture on the wall. It showed St. Martin in Roman uniform using his sword to cut his cloak for the beggar.

"That's what I saw!" cried the man.

"And you've never seen this picture before?"

"Never!"

"What you thought was a bow," my friend went on, "was the sword and the cloak. The picture was given you to show that you'd come to the right place to find help—to the church of Jesus Christ."

The confession of sins and the renunciation of evil are, then, two basic requirements for healing of any kind. The restoration of the ministry of healing in the church today has brought with it the need to help people come to repentance and deliverance so that nothing stands between them and God when prayer for healing is offered. For the healing of certain emotional hurts, however, more help is often needed before those wounded in this way can receive the grace of God; and it is to this aspect of ministry that we will now turn.

SEVEN

Out of the Depths

"INNER HEALING," "THE HEALING OF THE MEMORIES," and "prayer counseling" are a cluster of titles which have attached themselves to more or less the same form of ministry. To understand what is behind them, we have to consider the impact psychological medicine has made on the church in this century.

From a casual reading of the Gospels, Jesus might not have seemed much involved in psychology; but a closer study shows that he had a discerning awareness of what motivates women and men. He knew what was in the heart of man. It was out of men's hearts that "evil thoughts, fornication, theft, murder, adultery, coveting, wickedness, deceit, licentiousness, envy, slander, pride, foolishness" proceeds (Mk 7:21-22): a pretty comprehensive recital of the sins which spring from our personalities. So he spoke of the blessed, those who are "pure in heart" (Mt 5:8), because no trace of self-centeredness separates them from God.

"Heart" is one of the words in the Bible used to refer to that which controls our attitudes and conduct and which enables us to respond to the Spirit of God. "Soul," "spirit" and "mind" are also used: the Scriptures do not have a tidy psychological vocabulary. But it was the insight of the prophets to realize that if a man is going to be changed, it is his heart that has to be renewed, and that the only one who can accomplish such a change is God (Jer 24:7; Ez 36:26). That is why the devout Israelite prayed, "Create in me a clean heart, O God, and

97

put a new and right spirit within me" (Ps 51:10).

The apostolic writings insist that faith in Jesus Christ is only real when it results in a complete change of heart—what we call nowadays a radical reorientation of our personalities. It involves an inner death to self and a spiritual resurrection in Christ. This is what Paul meant when he wrote, "If you confess with your lips that Jesus is Lord and believe in your heart that God raised him from the dead, you will be saved. For man believes with his heart and so is justified, and he confesses with his lips and so is saved" (Rom 10:9-10). Those who have been set in a right relationship with God through repentance and faith in Jesus Christ will be saved (made whole, healed) because what they confess will not be a verbal claim with no substance in it but an expression of their total surrender to God.

Now many are not able to make this total surrender to God because they are inflicted with psychological problems which prevent this full giving of themselves. They require not only the forgiveness of sins but inner healing as well. The inner self needs making whole, just as the physical body does when it is sick.

What modern psychological studies have done is to offer us scientific charts through which we may trace the development or repression of our inner self. From the moment of birth—perhaps for some months before that—we are subjected to all kinds of pressures and tensions which affect the growth of our personalities; and as we move through each stage of life, infancy, childhood, adolescence, adulthood, middle age, and old age, fresh pressures and tensions arise from the sick world in which we live. It is said that a high proportion of beds in the hospitals of the Western world are occupied by those whose sicknesses are emotional or mental rather than physical. It is also said that many functional and organic illnesses are often indications of inward diseases.

Christians take this kind of study for granted these days, but this was not so in the early days of psychological medicine. Initially the new science was regarded with suspicion by the church. Because Sigmund Freud (d. 1939), the best-known pioneer in this field, pronounced religion to be a universal neurosis and God to be a fictitious projection, and then seemed to infer that, as human beings, we have no such thing as free will, Christians reacted with distaste and hostility to his work. His overwhelming emphasis on sexuality as the driving impulse of human conduct produced in the church a revulsion against his theories and his associated treatment techniques. It seemed as if he were doing nothing more than spreading immorality through a smokescreen of professional respectability.

Within a generation, however, other psychologists put forward ideas which respected the spiritual nature of man. Carl Jung (d. 1961) argued that God is not a substitute for a physical father but rather that a physical father is an infant's first substitute for God. Christian writers from different traditions—Victor White (Roman Catholic), Leonard Grensted (Anglican) and Leslie Weatherhead (Methodist), for example—advanced psychological theories more in tune with the church's own understanding of man and related them to traditional teaching and pastoral practice.

Since World War II there has grown up throughout the Christian world a considerable expansion of the counseling ministry, undertaken in the belief that whatever dark shadows may lie deep within our ego, superego, and id, the light of Christ can reach down and dispel them with his healing grace. A distinctly Christian contribution is being made to psychological medicine to show how man, in spite of his limitations and disturbances, is made in the image of God, to love God and to serve him and to enjoy him forever. There has been a mushrooming of societies, associations, and institutes to promote this ministry among clergy and laity alike. At times when pastors have become uncertain of their role in the church, they have often seized on counseling as an obviously useful task in a society which contains more and more unhappy souls.

But the Christian-sponsored counseling that developed often seemed little different from that which took place in any analyst's room. The Christians who engaged in it were certainly aware of God's love for their clients, but they did not look for God to intervene directly through the sessions. They probably never prayed with those who came to see them. Their aim was to help individuals to understand themselves better and to draw on their own resources and on those provided by supportive relationships until they were able to accept themselves as they really are.

Now this is, of course, a perfectly valid form of pastoral care. The counselor stands by his client and waits for the client's inner resources to be mobilized. Many have gone away from such sessions feeling more content than before; but some Christians feel that what they experience is less than the peace of Jesus Christ.

One of the deceptions of our times is that there are signs of peace which look attractive in themselves and which may indeed contain elements of God's goodness but which fall short of the real thing. Various systems are put forward for discovering more about ourselves. Advice is freely offered about assessing our relationships with others and about relating in a more friendly and helpful manner. Secular psychological therapy does enable many to live fuller lives. But can any healing be Christian healing if it does not result in a change of heart in the biblical sense? Can a man be whole without submitting inwardly to God's grace and accepting the Lordship of Christ in his life?

It was questions like these that led other Christians, particularly those involved in the new Pentecostal movement, to seek ways of invoking God's grace directly through prayer into people's painful memories and hurts from the past. Being more aware of the dynamic of the Holy Spirit in their own experience, they believed the same Spirit could renew the inner lives of troubled souls who opened themselves to God in faith.

So it was that the ministry of inner healing emerged. It was a process of reconstruction experienced under the guidance of the Holy Spirit. It did not attempt to supplant psychiatry, or to ignore the wisdom founded on secular psychology. It simply recognized that Jesus Christ, as the great physician, was interested in the healing of emotional trauma as well as physical disease; and that his commission to the church put his followers under an obligation to offer that ministry, too.

From Counseling to Prayer

Once the ministry of inner healing got under way, it was clear a vast area of human need was being uncovered. The circumstances under which contemporary women and men live impose enormous strains on them. Often clergy and laity were thrust into this ministry with little or no training. The development of groups in congregations provided countless opportunities for hidden hurts and emotional disturbances to rise to the surface of people's lives. Mistakes were made—plenty of them—but many found a new peace and personal renewal.

The need for this kind of ministry is signaled in different ways. Appearances can be deceptive. We meet someone who has an apparently happy and contented attitude towards life. In a group she or he might be the most amusing or the most helpful person present. It is only when we get to know them that we gradually come to realize that all is not well and that there are deep hurts and disturbances within them.

Sometimes a personal crisis will expose these. A breakdown, or a threatened breakdown, in relationships with a close relative or friend, a death, a sudden change in circumstances, the ending of a job, or the move from one community to another—any change which shakes the securities of people can bring to the surface signs that deep below is a hatred of self, an inability to trust anyone, a weird guilt complex, a repressed resentment, an anxiety about the present, or a fear about the future. Where these trouble the individual so deeply that he can no longer cope with the demands and opportunities of daily living, then it is likely that inner healing is necessary.

From the outset of such a ministry, it is important to establish where the client is in his spiritual pilgrimage. Some people have a faith that is strong enough for them to face fully the reality of the painful memories within them; others are at a stage where to re-experience past pains is more than they can face. The former believe that God's love for them is so strong that they can look at painful memories without fear and in faith see themselves loved by God in the midst of the previous suffering: since that love is stronger than the pain, then the fruit of the Spirit—love, joy, peace—can be known in the very memories that previously caused fear, guilt, and suffering. The latter are not able to do that until they are prepared to step out in faith.

What is remarkable in this ministry of inner healing is that God, in answer to prayer, frequently gives the necessary faith just at the moment when the person requires it. Prayer for such faith is therefore an essential preliminary. Only then should the one who ministers seek to discern when to call forth specific memories, so that he can ask the Lord in the power of the Spirit to take the client back to that point in his life where the painful memories originated, and to touch him with healing love.

After a period of counseling, the minister will often invite his client to join him in a prayer which begins when the client was a fetus in the womb. Slowly the minister takes the client forward in time through birth and various stages of life, walking with him in imagination as one memory succeeds another. Sometimes the memory of a particular event will be so vivid to the client that he will begin to speak as if he were reliving it again.

"How old are you?" says the minister.

"Eleven," replies the client.

"Where are you?"

"In my father's garden."

"What are you doing?"

"Trying to hide."

"Why are you trying to hide?"

"Because I'm afraid."

"Who are you afraid of?"

The client is silent, but a struggle is going on inside him . . .

Some memories are not far below the surface. They usually originated in a single embarrassing or painful occasion which left the individual feeling guilty or fearful. A client like this can be helped by the minister to confess what is sinful and to invoke the love of God back to that occasion.

Other memories are much deeper. Frequently they are hidden beneath a confusing cluster of impressions and thoughts which the client has collected unconsciously round the deep pain to obliterate it and nullify the effects it has on him. Over the course of many sessions the minister will be presented with these surface impressions and thoughts and he will have to discern that they are really secondary, a sort of smokescreen to prevent him seeing the more distressing memories underneath.

There is no set pattern for this ministry. The only orthodoxy is that those involved should be constantly open to the leading of the Holy Spirit. Counselors learn from one another. Some choose to minister by themselves because they feel that a more trusting relationship can be established on a one-to-one basis. Others prefer to work in pairs so that one partner can take the initiative while the other prays. If those who minister together are a man and a woman—perhaps a husband and wife—they complement each other with their own distinctive insights.

In this ministry 1 Corinthians 12:8 becomes relevant: "To one is given through the Spirit the utterance of wisdom, and to another the utterance of knowledge according to the same Spirit." Commentators are not agreed precisely what Paul meant by these *charismata*; but in the ministry of inner healing these spiritual gifts can be important. "The utterance of wisdom" is interpreted as a revelation from God which has a direct bearing on the counseling session as it is in progress: in prayer, one of those involved is inspired to say something which has an enlightening and reassuring effect on the client, even though it is rarely related to anything that has been said during the session. "The utterance of knowledge" is interpreted as a piece of information from God about the client which the counselors would not have discovered through the ordinary means of question and answer. "Sanctified hunches" is a cruder way of describing them.

Inner healing can be ministered in a group, although this requires experienced leadership and trusting relationships within the group itself to start with. The same conditions and safeguards apply as when a group is involved in a deliverance ministry—submission to pastoral authority, spiritual preparation, and practical follow-up.

I should point out, however, that not all Christians accept the validity of this kind of ministry. They argue that what is called inner healing is merely a manipulative technique induced by fantasies, that people are seduced by it because it seems to offer a shortcut to normal psychiatric treatment, and that it is fundamentally sub-Christian visualization and guided imagery masquerading under a veneer of scriptural phraseology. One or two go so far as to attack it as downright evil, on a par with occultism.

The only answer to these objections is to study the results. If through the ministry of inner healing an individual begins to show signs of a more mature life, manifesting the fruit of the Spirit in relationships with others—love, joy, peace, patience, kindness, goodness, faithfulness and self-control—then it is spiritual blindness to claim that such healing is not of God.

Yet this is not to say that every ministry of inner healing is equally successful. Nor is it to say that everyone who attempts to exercise this ministry is guided infallibly by the Holy Spirit. To this extent the critics are justified in uttering warnings.

An Imaginary Case

I think it would be helpful at this point if I asked you to join me in an imaginary counseling session to illustrate what I have been describing. Let us assume that we have been approached by a young man whom we do not know very well, and that we have fixed an appointment to see him in our home.

We prepare for this appointment beforehand by praying together and perhaps by undertaking a simple fast. We inform the prayer group we belong to (or friends in the congregation) about the appointment so that they can pray for us, too. What little we know about the young man can give substance to our intercessions for him, but we must beware of not letting our thoughts run away with us, so that we believe we know what he is coming to see us about and what advice we are going to give him! Once we've prayed, it's best to forget about him until the time for the appointment arrives.

We arrange that in the session I will take the initiative and you will observe and pray (and take a few notes, if he doesn't mind; they will be useful if we have to meet him a second time).

When we keep the appointment, our first task will be to help him to feel at ease with us. Much will depend on what relationship we already have with him. If we've known him for years, our starting point will be different than if he's a comparative stranger. We must show by our attitude that we are willing to share his problem with him and that we have no intention of being judgmental about it. If we are sincere about this, he will sense it and his self-consciousness will soon evaporate.

We avoid asking too many questions. We don't want the session to develop into a cut-and-thrust interrogation. Any questions we ask are designed to clarify the information we are receiving about his feelings or the facts he is telling us. We want to bring him to the point where he can talk to us freely without prompting or probing.

Although you and I have agreed that I should take the initiative, you occasionally make a comment or ask a question, so that our young man doesn't become uneasy about your silence; and now and then we make a comment to one another so that it doesn't seem too much of a two-to-one affair.

The session moves through stages.

First, we have to help him to accept that his present distress is caused by the things he has experienced in the past. He may find this difficult to understand or admit. Sometimes people's experience of the present is so overwhelming that it blots out everything else; they are swamped by what they are feeling now. For a time he may not even be able to see that the past has any relevance at all.

Or it could be that his present distress has its origins in some relationship which now makes him feel guilty and wretched and full of self-hatred. If that relationship involved, say, one of his parents, he may be unwilling to admit his feelings because that would seem rank disloyalty to the parent concerned (especially if that parent is dead). He may have unconsciously buried those feelings under layers of forgetfulness or substitute memories which we have to help him uncover.

Next, he has to face the pain of recalling those bitter or suppressed memories. This is the next part of the struggle. He would much rather keep them out of his mind. He may tell us stories to head us off when we seem to be getting close. We have to help him to realize that the path to his healing is through the memories of emotional and mental pain. By recalling them honestly and fully, he is making a sacrifice of them to God—offering them up, so that through the love and power of Jesus Christ their effects on him can be broken and the experience of them transfigured into a means of growth and maturity.

It is not uncommon to have to go over the same facts several times in succeeding sessions (this is where our notes come in handy). To us, as counselors, this may seem an unnecessary repetition; but to our client it is extremely important—it may be the only way in which he can be helped to face the past. He accepts a little bit more each time until he has accepted all of it.

While he is telling his story, we ask the Holy Spirit for those gifts which will enable us to discern those memories which are related to his present problem and reveal the cause of them. We let him tell his story in his own time; the way he tells it may provide us with valuable clues about his own attitudes and fears. And, as we listen, ideas and impressions begin to crowd into our minds.

Inwardly we ask the Lord for the gift of discernment. We note each idea and impression, but we don't dwell on them. We file them away in a mental filing cabinet, asking the Spirit to recall them individually if and when it is appropriate to do so. We have to be on our guard against letting our attentions wander. It's easily done. He says something. Yes, we say inwardly to ourselves, I had a similar trouble when I was about that age. I remember it turned out to be . . . Suddenly we are no longer listening—or ministering.

We ask a few questions about those times in his life, when, like all of us, he was particularly vulnerable to emotional injury, and about those relationships he had with those closest to him, like the ones just mentioned. Separations, illnesses, deaths, and other tragedies among these people may have affected his sense of being loved. They often cause hidden wounds, the effects of which only manifest themselves later. Slowly a picture of the life of this young man is built up; and it is humbling to realize that perhaps no other human being has seen that life in quite the same way that we do. We have been given the privilege of looking into the heart of another, in order to be the Lord's ministers in bringing healing and peace.

After a period of listening, we watch for the Holy Spirit to provide us with an opportunity to pray together. Quite often the client himself senses when that moment has come. We tell him to sit in a relaxed and expectant manner (he may have been leaning forward tensely). We sit in a relaxed and expectant manner, too. A minute or two's silence. You read out a passage of Scripture which came into your head.

Then I get up and stand beside him while you sit near him on his other side. Together we concentrate on listening to the voice of the Spirit. I begin to pray aloud; you join in occasionally with a petition, or another verse of Scripture, or in sharing a thought you've had. Our prayer goes over the facts that have been presented to us from each phase of the young man's life. We ask him to recall each phase in his imagination as we pray and live them afresh, in the spirit of prayer, as far as he is able. It may be that during the prayer he remembers further incidents or additional details of things he has told us already; these, too, we incorporate into the prayer.

During the session we realized that a bond with a parent was particularly painful because the normal emotions of attachment had been distorted through the way the relationship developed in our client's early years. In Jesus' name we command that the bond be broken, and then we invoke the Holy Spirit to heal and renew the relationship so that the bond is one of natural love which no longer causes pain. The young man reacts with a spasm of weeping as we pray like this, so we wait until he has calmed down before we continue.

Finally, we suggest he ask God for the forgiveness and healing of any pain which he may have caused others. It is a sign that inner healing is beginning to take place when a person can be less concerned about himself and more concerned about what he might have done to others. Indeed, if the ministry accomplishes what we hope and pray for, it will result in a new inner dying to self and spiritual rising in Christ for service to others as a disciple of Jesus. Our time of devotion ends with an act of praise and thanksgiving.

We check with the young man either that he will keep in touch with us in case he requires further help, or that he is in contact with a group of Christians who can continue to pray with him and support him over the next few months. The following Sunday we report to the pastor of our congregation briefly what we have done. The pastor may advise us about training in counseling to help us in this ministry, or he may put us in touch with one or two others who have had more experience than we have, to guide us if the case gets more complicated later on.

We have to recognize that some people's problems may be too difficult for us to handle. The fact that we have helped this young man does not qualify us to take on anyone who may approach us!

The basis for our partnership in ministry to others for inner healing is as follows:

1. Accepting one another as gifted by the Holy Spirit for this ministry together, recognizing that one will take the initiative while the other will take a supporting role.

2. The involvement of a local group of Christians who will pray for us.

3. Our submission to the pastoral leadership of the congregation to which we belong.

4. Our willingness to accept (a) the guidance of those more experienced than ourselves, and (b) appropriate forms of training in spiritual and psychological subjects, even if this only takes the form of directed reading.

5. Our total surrender to the Lordship of Jesus Christ and our commitment to him and his love for those who come to us with deep emotional needs.

From Darkness to Light

"God is light and in him is no darkness at all" (1 Jn 1:5). The biblical imagery of darkness and light applies in a vivid way to the ministries of deliverance and inner healing. The impulses and wounds from the deep conscious, coupled sometimes with evil influences, have all the characteristics of darkness. Indeed, individuals who are emotionally sick seem to have a darkness within them that casts its shadow around them. Notice how a severely depressed person seems to infect with gloom those he is with.

Then, in this as in any form of ministry to others, we have to cope with the darkness within ourselves. Ministry to others throws strains on us, too. We find ourselves reacting against certain personalities. They make us feel uncomfortable or irritable. We have to learn that reactions like these come from unresolved tensions and anxieties within ourselves. We need wisdom to recognize when we cannot minister to others because we have not yet allowed the Lord to banish all the darkness in our own lives. Maybe they need someone with greater experience, or a qualified psychiatrist. Two important lessons are discerning whom we cannot help and guiding them to those who can.

The objective of inner healing is to enable us to participate *freely* and *willingly* in the life of God through Jesus Christ in the power of the Holy Spirit. If our response to God is twisted or thwarted by problems deep within ourselves, then it will not be free and willing. We might say that inner healing is a ministry which encourages us to turn from self-absorption to self-oblation.

For at every stage of our spiritual pilgrimage we shall, if we try to walk in the Spirit, find the cross in some shape or form. Christ's saying about losing life in order to gain it applies from the beginning to the end of our Godward journey. To undertake the Christian pilgrimage, then, we have to come to that point where we can surrender ourselves inwardly to God knowing that, whatever demands might be made on us, his grace is sufficient for us. We are healed in order that we may no longer seek a futile self-confidence but that we might be spiritually reborn into a rock-like confidence in Jesus Christ. We can know the forgiveness of God in our hearts, and we can enter into relationships with others, especially those in the Christian community, with that openness which enables the Holy Spirit to use us as members of the body of Christ. "If we walk in the light, as he is in the light, we have fellowship with one another, and the blood of Jesus his Son cleanses us from all sin" (1 Jn 1:7).

EIGHT

Beloved Physicians

YOU ONLY HAVE TO WALK THROUGH a large hospital to be
reminded what an enormous ministry of healing is exercised
through those institutions. A clergyman who visits one of his flock in
an intensive-care unit can feel as much out of place as an atheist in a
mosque during Ramadan. Alongside the curing and caring that is
organized through public and private health services, what the
church has to offer can seem very puny indeed. Just a few folk prayed
with, just a few of those healed—that's all.

In any country where Christians are a minority in the population,
the proportion of the sick who will look to the church for healing is
bound to be small. The doctor with his white coat and stethoscope
and the nurse with her tray of drugs have become the symbols of
healing in the popular mind, not the Christian congregation at
prayer with the laying on of hands and anointing. In third world
countries which are experiencing rapid church growth, this is not the
case. Where medical services are far less sophisticated and where
people are less dependent on the importations of Western civilization, the church's sacramental and charismatic ministries of
healing are more widely accepted. And, apparently, with a higher
success rate than in Western countries. Those who have studied this
phenomenon suggest that in our modern world we have become so
mentally and emotionally dependent on scientific and technological
solutions to our problems that we are almost incapable of seeking

111

spiritual and communal resources for healing.

Although much healing comes through the work of hospitals, they are no less prone than other institutions to the danger of moving towards the tyrannical rather than towards the humane in their use of new techniques. Christians and others who labor in them find themselves in a constant struggle not to treat the sick as less than human beings. The technological advances of recent decades have engendered a tendency to treat a patient's body as a machine subject to malfunctioning. A hospital chaplain listed the unspoken and unarticulated assumptions which, he believed, determined much of what went on in a hospital:

1. The cure of the disease is more important than the care of the patient.
2. The staff assume power over the patients.
3. Individuals are separate from one another.
4. The provision of health is a task for the experts.
5. Every problem has a solution.
6. Death is the worst thing that can happen to a person.

He went on to draw a picture of the hospital as an institution whose organization and functioning is complicated by relationships between specialists with their support structures, various services with their own hierarchies, competition for prized status positions, and differing lines of communication. In the midst of it all is the patient, he said, more like a victim of the system than the one for whom the system exists.

How far that chaplain was justified in making those comments about his own particular hospital it is, of course, impossible to say; but from what I have observed and heard I suspect there is a good deal of truth in them. It isn't that people don't care. It's because the institution exerts its own strange influence over its members, often blinding them to the reality which the chaplain discerned. With such discernment (a gift of the Spirit), the church has a mission to challenge such unspoken and unarticulated assumptions and expose them for what they are: contrary to the gospel of Jesus Christ.

For it is a fundamental tenet of the gospel that we are created by God and made in his image. It was in a human body that Christ, having died, was raised and now reigns as man as well as God. Hence human bodies are sacred: they are fashioned to be temples of the Holy Spirit and, in the mercy of God, to be resurrected in their glorified state with Christ in the kingdom of heaven. A person's body cannot be separated from his total being. We are integrated personalities of which our physical nature is a constituent element.

Within the world of medicine, therefore, as in other sectors of our modern society, the church has an important task in upholding the human dignity of the sick and the value of their relationships with others. Alongside her own ministry to them through prayer and sacrament, the church must demonstrate the love of the Savior by *reverencing* those who are ill and encouraging others involved in their care to do the same.

How this care is expressed can cause frictions between the church and the medical profession. Abortion and euthanasia are two obvious areas, but problems arise over a wide variety of developments—the ability to prolong life by artificial means, new techniques in transplant operations, genetic engineering and *in vitro* fertilization, and advances in endocrinology and neurosurgery where treatments can have far-reaching effect on the personality.

Difficult decisions have to be made about priorities in hospitals. Almost all forms of cure cost an enormous amount of money. The bill for certain research and techniques is astronomical. What are the ethical implications of the choices that have to be made? Should money be spent on heart transplants for the few or on routine operations for the many? Should limited resources be concentrated on the aged sick or on the young injured? Then it is necessary to seek the deeper motives behind the decisions that are made. Has a choice been made for the benefit of the patients or for the prestige of the institution? Has the newly created post in the research department really been focused on a growing need or on a sparkling reputation?

The church leader who is expected to make pronouncements on such matters has an unenviable task when he encounters the medical world with its intricate technology and jargon. The speed of some developments is so swift that there is little chance for the nonexpert to keep up to date. In fact, it is the vital ministry of Christians who are actually working in the health services to help the church to see what is truly of God's healing grace among these complex ethical issues. As a community within the hospital service, they are uniquely situated to aid in the discerning process. The chaplain has a privileged position as a theologically trained pastor standing by them in the struggle against pain and disease.

If the church has to challenge the unspoken and unarticulated assumptions of the hospital and the secular health services, then she must be prepared to show that there are better ways. Take, for example, the sixth item on the list above. The Christian cannot agree that death is always the worst thing that can happen to a person. Death can be tragically untimely, and everything that does not dehumanize a patient must be done to preserve release and a healing. To demonstrate this, some Christians have in the years since World War II established the hospice movement with its care of the terminally ill. A careful use of drugs to relieve pain is part of the care, but more vital is the atmosphere of the hospice, with its sense of community among staff and patients and its over-arching hope in the mercy of God.

Although there may sometimes be friction between the church and the medical profession, there are many signs nowadays that others besides Christians are well aware of these problems. Ethical issues are much discussed in medical and nursing circles, and they are the subject of innumerable articles and letters in professional journals and popular magazines. The hospital's ethical committee is one of many institutional safeguards against abuse. But there is also more attention not just to what is done but to how it is done.

There is much talk about holistic medicine, about treating the whole person in body, mind, and spirit, not merely the symptoms. What an individual thinks and feels, his hopes and fears, his relations with others, his attitude towards life in general—that these are widely recognized factors in any illness and need to be taken into account when he presents himself to the doctor for diagnosis and treatment. Recovery is aided when a patient understands and accepts his condition and gains confidence that someone can help him. Clearly this is very relevant to the relationship between medical and nursing care and the church's ministry of healing.

I visited an elderly relative in the hospital one Sunday afternoon. She was due to have an operation the following day. Although she put a brave face on her situation, she was naturally apprehensive. While I was sitting by her bed, the surgeon came into the ward and approached her. He was in ordinary clothes and had apparently taken time on his day off to see the patients he was to operate on the next day. He explained simply to my relative what the operation was for and how she would feel when she came round from the general anaesthetic. Before he went on to his next patient, he took her hand and said, "We're going to set you on the road to recovery tomorrow." The effect on her was remarkable. Her apprehension vanished; she became lively and cheerful. I prayed with her before I left, but I felt my prayers were but a thanksgiving for a healing process which had begun through the surgeon's visit.

From Cooperation to Integration

One element in restoring the church's ministry of healing is in strengthening the cooperation between the church and medicine so that there is an integration of medical and nursing care with the sacramental and charismatic ministry offered by the Christian community. This looks much more feasible with the convergence between the medical concern for holistic care and the Christian concern for total healing. In the light of the church's history, another name for holistic medicine could be pastoral care.

To illustrate what I mean by moving from cooperation to integration, I will briefly describe a few examples from different parts of the world, taken from my personal knowledge or from reports I have seen. I will list them so that they show varying degrees of cooperation.

My first example comes from London.

St. Marylebone is the parish church of Harley Street. Its clergy serve as chaplains to seven hospitals. Three great teaching hospitals are just over its parochial boundaries. More medicine is practiced in these few acres than in any equivalent area in the world. Yet, by a strange quirk of inner city life, it is difficult for an ordinary resident to enroll with a local general practitioner as a national health patient.

It was factors like these which prompted the parish church to launch an appeal to convert the crypt under its huge building into a health and healing center. Firms of builders and funeral directors worked to clear out the coffins of the gentry which had been crammed into every available space from 1817, when the church was built, to 1850, when the crypt was sealed off. The crypt has now been redeveloped to provide, among other facilities, consulting rooms from two national health general practitioners, a nurse, and a health visitor, alongside counseling rooms and office for the clergy. The Churches' Council for Health and Healing and other national agencies have their offices in the center. Weekly services of healing have been established in the church.

St. Marylebone is particularly interesting because it demonstrates what can be done where most patients are treated under a national health service. There are similar projects in other parts of Britain. In countries where private health services are more widespread, or where health care is available through voluntary or charitable schemes, the degree of integration can be greater.

My second example comes from a report published in 1982 in the United States, the results of a research project by Thomas A. Droege on the healing ministry exercised in eight Lutheran congregations. Entitled *Ministry to the Whole Person* (Valparaiso University, Indiana), it showed the considerable variety in the ways this ministry is developing from one church to another, yet all with cooperation of the medical and related professions.

In Trinity Church, Minneapolis, a comprehensive health center provides a program of health care under the direction of a professional care team which includes a doctor, a nurse, and a counselor. In another city, a preventive scheme is administered through the educational structures of a congregation and its school, with an emphasis on assuming personal responsibility for one's own health and lifestyle. In other cities, a variety of both preventive and curative personal ministries for older persons has developed. But one of the most striking projects is in Faith Lutheran Church, Geneva, Illinois, about forty miles west of Chicago.

Faith Church was established in a largely white, middle-class area in 1963, and about ten years later began to experience a spiritual renewal through the influence of a group of new Pentecostals. As the renewal developed and matured, lay people became involved in various ministries, accepting careful training and supervision. What impressed Dr. Droege was the way in which the various ministries in the congregation are fulfilled with a high level of awareness that God is at the center of their lives, and with a sensitive determination to meet human need in whatever form it appears.

The congregation is organized under an eldership scheme. Each elder is responsible for a certain number of families. Groups are called together to help with the care of those with special needs. It is within this pattern that the healing ministry is developing. The elders meet the pastor regularly each week for prayer and discussion, and they lead the healing ministry both within the congregation and beyond it. It is symbolic of their ministry that each elder has a vial of olive oil in his personal possession—one of them keeps it on his key chain.

There is a monthly service of prayer for healing which attracts people from a wide area. These visitors are ministered to for spiritual problems, counseling, inner healing, and deliverance. But increasingly the ministry is being more closely integrated with the congregation's worship and life. People can be prayed for at any time in a service or a meeting. The church has produced its own *Healing Ministry Team Manual,* and the elders and others involved are encouraged to keep up to date with their studies, which include consultations with doctors and psychiatrists.

The degree of lay involvement impressed the author of the report, Dr. Droege:

> Most pastors affirm the idea of lay ministry, but such ministry is usually limited to Sunday School teaching, committee work, and chores like ushering and counting the money. But the ministry in this church is a ministry to human need, and the amount of energy which is generated within the congregation towards meeting that need is impressive.

He admitted that he was not a new Pentecostal himself. This made it difficult for him to enter into certain aspects of the renewal movement. But he hoped this also meant he could be objective in his assessment of what he encountered.

He concluded:

> It seems to me that this model (of a healing ministry at Faith Church) comes nearer than any others in this study to the biblical method and theology of healing. The method is patterned after the method used by Jesus, his disciples, and the early church: prayer, laying on of hands, and anointing with oil. The theology of healing is also thoroughly biblical. There is an emphasis on God's promise to heal and encouragement to trust that promise. There is recognition in practice as well as in theory that the church's mission is to heal as well as to preach.

My third example illustrating how cooperation becomes almost integration is at the Bethel Baptist Church in Kingston, Jamaica. A healing center has been established which includes a medical clinic, a counseling department, a telephone ministry, and a prayer room. A team of doctors, pharmacists, counselors, and nurses, together with clerical and maintenance staff, gives their services free to enable the center to be open two or more evenings each week. Those with a ministry of prayer for the sick take it in turn to man the prayer room all the time the center is open. They not only keep a vigil of intercession but they also minister to individuals who are referred to them by others on the staff in the center.

Individuals who come to the center are first screened in a brief interview to determine which department they should be referred to. It is also explained to them that they might be referred not only to a doctor or a pharmacist but also to a counselor or a prayer partner. Non-medical and previously inexperienced lay people from the congregation act as the doctor's assistants. If a doctor feels that an individual needs more medical treatment than the center can offer, that individual is sent on to a hospital. Trained counselors are also available for those with psychological problems.

The doctors are encouraged to devote fifteen minutes to each patient. This puts a strain on the waiting list, but the center believes a holistic approach to each case demands that kind of attention if consultations are not to become hurried and impersonal. The staff accepts as a limitation that it will not be able to cope with as many patients as it could if it dealt with each case from a purely medical angle; it prefers to offer a ministry to the whole person for the restoration of full health.

As a fourth example, I have heard of an even more integrated medical and spiritual ministry which has been developed by the Kimbanguist Church in its clinics and hospitals in Zaire. This church was founded by a Baptist catechist, Simon Kimbangu, who began an extensive preaching and healing ministry in 1921, attracting great crowds. The movement alarmed the Belgian authorities, who believed it might turn into a political insurrection, so they arrested Kimbangu, tried him, and condemned him to death. The sentence was later commuted to life imprisonment, and the prisoner was exiled to Shaba where he died in 1951. Those who followed him became the "Church of Jesus Christ on Earth through the Prophet

Simon Kimbangu." In spite of persecution the Kimbanguists grew to become the largest indigenous church in Africa today.

When Western missionaries first encountered the Kimbanguist Church in what was then the Belgian Congo, they were sceptical about the stories of miraculous healings which they heard were performed in that church. But over the years they came to recognize that this was a form of ministry which Christians in the West had neglected. In modern times Kimbanguists have maintained their ministry of prayer with the laying on of hands and incorporated it into the care of the sick in their health clinics and hospitals.

Visitors describe how the two overlap. No Kimbanguist doctor begins the exercise of his function unless he has joined in a prayer meeting with the medical personnel under him. Once a month choirs go in turn to the hospitals and clinics to sing and pray for the patients. Prayers are said daily in the morning, at midday, and in the evening. The visits organized by Kimbanguist prayer groups make it possible for patients not only to receive moral and spiritual support but also material assistance as far as resources permit. The church makes use of these opportunities to proclaim the gospel, and as a result many pagans ask to be baptized before they leave the hospital or the clinic.

Celebration

These examples of cooperation might leave the impression that the church's only concern is to persuade the medical and nursing professions that their work can be within the orbit of the church's pastoral ministry if they go about it conscious of their Christian discipleship. But there is much in modern scientific medicine and nursing care that we, as the church, can thank God for as well. "Every good endowment and every perfect gift is from above" (Ja 1:17). While healing in a Christian's eyes cannot be moving towards completion unless it draws those involved closer to God, yet we can still celebrate what is truly of God in all that is done for the sick and disabled which helps them to live more fully as human beings.

There has been a curious reluctance among some in the church to acknowledge that those of other faiths or of no faith can in any way be instruments of the Lord in his healing work. Can those who do not recognize Jesus as their Savior and Lord be linked even distantly with a Christian ministry?

I can understand why the question is asked. Superficially it does seem strange to suggest that a surgeon who is by conviction a humanist can be acting as a minister of the church's pastoral concern for the sick when he performs an operation. But if he is motivated by a desire to relieve suffering among his fellow human beings, then that is good; and where goodness is manifested in the dealings women and men have with one another, God's grace is behind it somewhere, even if unacknowledged by them. The Holy Spirit is not bound by Christians' confession of faith. The Bible has many examples of the way God used those who did not know him. And sometimes we can be so eager to see miraculous healings that we don't see the wonderful healings achieved by medical science.

To celebrate what is truly of God in secular health care is one important element in restoring the church's healing ministry. It gives encouragement and guidance to Christians who work in those health services, and it enables Christians who undergo medical treatment to offer themselves and those who treat them to the Lord. The highly scientific and busy atmosphere of a modern hospital often seems light years away from the Christian community in which our faith is nurtured, and Christian doctors and nurses often have a difficult task not to keep their professional work and their personal faith in separate compartments of their lives.

Yet if the Lord is our healer, he is also in the wards, in the operating room, in the laboratories and the other departments of a medical center, as well as in the chapel where a few gather for the midweek communion service. The Christian in such establishments should not need crucifixes and religious pictures about the place to remind him of this (although they can be helpful in hospitals and nursing homes with Christian foundations). The Lord is present in all that is done through a genuine concern to cure disease.

How a Christian doctor or nurse witnesses to Jesus Christ within what is required of them professionally is for each individual to discern for herself or himself. One or two Christian surgeons had a reputation for summoning the operating room staff for prayer at the beginning of a day's work (though I suspect that was easier in the past than it is today); Christian nurses have occasionally laid hands on a particular patient and briefly prayed with him (behind the curtains). But the heart of Christian witness lies in the way we do our jobs and the relationships we establish with others in the process.

It seems to me that open involvement with the church's ministry of healing begins for the professionals as it does for all other Christians—within the congregation of which they are members. If doctors and nurses take their appropriate part in the prayer and other forms of ministry offered for the sick in their local church, then they will begin to see how that ministry overflows into their professional dealing with their patients and colleagues.

In recent years I've noticed a small but growing number of medics joining in services of prayer for healing—and occasionally seeking that ministry for their own ailments. Recently I presided over such a service. There were about a hundred in the congregation, a dozen of whom came forward for prayer and the laying on of hands. Afterwards two people came to talk to me. One was an eye surgeon, the other was a family practitioner; both wanted to know more about the ministry of healing and both asked if, next time there was a service, they could join the prayer and the laying on of hands. This is a further example of how spiritual renewal strengthens the church's ministry: both these doctors had been influenced by the new Pentecostal movement.

Professional roles in clinics and hospitals make it difficult for Christian medical staff to be overtly involved in this form of ministry in those places; but in their own congregations it soon becomes accepted that doctors and nurses are fitting members of the team which prays with the sick. It seems just as appropriate as, say, it is for an accountant to act as church treasurer.

I had been asked to preach in a small church situated in what was once a village but is now a sprawling suburb. When I arrived about fifteen minutes before the service was due to begin, the pastor led me to the vestry.

"It's the first Sunday of the month," he said, "and we usually offer prayer with the laying on of hands to anyone who wants ministry. Would you like to do it this evening?"

"How many usually come up?" I asked.

"Not more than ten or a dozen. They come up to the communion rail during the hymn after the sermon, and you can pray for them there."

"Yes, I'll do it," I replied, "but I'd rather share in the ministry with someone else. I feel that shows it's a ministry of the church as a whole and not just of an individual. Will you do it with me?"

The pastor thought for a moment.

"I'll ask the lay reader to do it with you," he said. "He's taking the service tonight. I'll stay in my seat for a change."

I left the vestry to arrange my Bible and notes in the pulpit. When I returned, the pastor and the choir were lined up ready to enter the church. I just had time to shake hands briefly with the reader—a pleasant, elderly man—before taking my place in the procession.

The reader led the service very competently, and I preached. When I came down from the pulpit, the reader beckoned me to follow him into the sanctuary.

"We'll both lay hands on each person," I whispered. "I'll say the prayer over the first, you over the second, and so on."

He nodded.

Eight people came up and knelt at the communion rail. I asked the first, a woman, what she wanted us to pray for; then I placed my hands gently on her head and prayed in a quiet voice. I was conscious that the reader had put a hand on her shoulder as I did so.

We moved to the next person. I felt slightly anxious. Partnering a complete stranger in this kind of ministry is not easy. You can never be sure what they'll say! Will they make a complete mess of it so that you have to take over? I put my hand on the shoulder of the next one and braced myself.

To my delight, the reader prayed beautifully. He obviously knew the person we were ministering to; he used scriptural phrases with reverent ease and his words expressed the loving concern of God.

I relaxed. This man was discerning and sensitive to the leading of the Spirit. I have to confess that for the rest of the ministry I paid more attention to the prayers he offered than to the needs of those kneeling before us.

By the time I had shaken hands with the members of the congregation after the service and returned to the vestry, the reader was already about to leave. He shook hands with me, said he had enjoyed my sermon, and disappeared out of the door.

When we were alone, I remarked to the pastor how well the reader had prayed for those who had come forward.

"Yes, he always does," said the pastor. "Bill's done a good deal to encourage us to follow up the ministry of healing in this church. In fact, if it hadn't been for him, we certainly wouldn't have done what you did and he did tonight. I was far too sceptical in the early days!"

"What's his job?" I asked.

The pastor smiled. "He's our local doctor," he replied.

From that night the words "beloved physician" took on a richer meaning for me.

NINE

The Prayer of Faith

W HEN THE PEOPLE OF GOD ARE TOUCHED afresh by the Holy
Spirit, they are given a greater desire to pray. It's not that they
find praying any easier. Usually far from it—if my experience is
anything like that of others.' But prayer becomes infinitely more
worthwhile, for they sense the Spirit moving within them, drawing
them into a closer union with the Father through Jesus Christ.

And since the church's ministry of healing is essentially one of
prayer, that ministry is also renewed through the Spirit's moving.

But how should we pray for the sick?

There's always a tendency for us to treat prayer for the sick as if it
were more like a magical formula than an act of spiritual communion
with God. We get the idea that so-and-so's prayer is more effective
than ours because his relationship with God is different and he
knows just the right words to use. We are tempted to try to
manipulate the Lord through our prayers rather than let him
manipulate us.

We have to remember that there is no privileged hierarchy in the
people of the new covenant. Christ is our one high priest. United in
him, each of us can approach the throne of grace. Any of us can pray
for healing—for ourselves and for others.

Misunderstandings can arise out of a careless reading of passages
like James 5:16; "The prayer of a righteous man has great power in its
effects." Superficially that sounds as if the more holy an intercessor

is, the more likely it is that God will hear his prayer.

Now I don't want to underplay the importance of personal holiness in any ministry. Obviously those who are more obedient to the Lord are more likely to pray according to his will. And it is, of course, perfectly scriptural to ask for others to pray for you, especially those whom you believe are trying to be faithful disciples of Christ. But when he used the phrase "a righteous man," the author of James was echoing the assurances in Old Testament passages such as Psalm 34:15 and Proverbs 15:29, which teach that God hears the prayers of those who trust him. What he was saying was that those to whom his letter was addressed should have confidence in the efficacy of prayer, provided the prayers they offered were not just words of half-hearted utterances but petitions which sprang from their trust in God. Such prayers would be powerful because they would be inspired by the power which God gives.

Prayer for the sick should be "in the Spirit." That is why traditional forms of prayer end with some variation of the words, "Through Jesus Christ our Lord, who lives and reigns with you, Father, and the Holy Spirit." This phrase and others like it are so familiar to us that we tend to rattle them off without a thought. Yet it enshrines the New Testament teaching on the nature of prayer—that it is offered in and through Jesus Christ who, by the operation of the Holy Spirit, redeems us and sanctifies us and makes our prayers acceptable to God. Prayer is the Spirit of God praying in us.

Formal prayers can be useful as models, such as this one:

O merciful God,
giver of life and health;
bless, we pray, your servant
and those who minister to him of your healing gifts:
that he may be restored to health of body and mind;
through Jesus Christ our Lord.

But most of us would probably prefer something more personal and spontaneous. We would want to incorporate into what we say things about the sickness and the situation of the person we are praying for. Which means we have to rely on what the Holy Spirit puts into our minds at the time rather than on the text of a prayer from a book.

Now I can't instruct you in detail how to do this. The effectiveness of your own prayer for a sick individual will depend on many things—not least on the degree of openness you and those around you have to God when you pray. But I can list certain ingredients in this ministry of prayer for healing which the Holy Spirit uses to guide us when we pray.

1. Attention to the Scriptures

We come to know God and enter into a relationship with him through the Bible with the enlightening of the Holy Spirit. The word of God is a living word, addressed to us now, a word which brings us eternal life. Prayer for the sick, therefore, finds its inspiration from what the Bible teaches about God's will and our obedience as his disciples. This will profoundly influence what we pray and how we say it.

But the Scriptures can also inspire our prayer for the sick more directly through the use we make of a passage.

A biblical text can be used in two ways for prayer:

—It can be read aloud slowly, followed by silence and a comment or two, letting the message and its meaning sink into the minds and hearts of those who hear it.

—Its key words and phrases can be incorporated into the prayers which are said with the sick person.

The first is a meditative use of the text; the second is a verbal use of it. Quite often, the two uses run together.

We don't just have to use the stories of the healings in the Gospels and in Acts. Accounts of the words and deeds of Jesus are highly suitable; so, too, are the promises of God and the declarations of faith in the Old and the New Testaments. Passages of thanksgiving and praise from the apostolic writings can be encouraging. But of all the books in the Bible, the Psalms often speak to and for a sick person with a startling relevance, for the psalmist takes all our moods, our frustrations, and our sense of helplessness, and helps us to seek God's grace to change our feelings into faith, hope, and love.

A friend of mine was rushed to the hospital after he had had a heart attack. He was kept in an intensive-care unit for several days. A devout Roman Catholic, he had taken with him a prayer book and used it to read the Psalms, Bible passages, canticles, and collects appointed for each day. He told me afterwards that while he was in the unit, the Scriptures sprang to life for him in a way he had never known before.

"The Psalms, especially," he said, "seemed to stand out from the page and give me the prayers I felt I needed."

He quoted verses which, he felt, were particularly appropriate for him (my italics): "For I am poor and needy, / and my *heart* is stricken within me. . . . / Help me, O Lord my God! / Save me according to thy steadfast love!" (Ps. 109:22,26). "I give thee thanks, O Lord, with my whole *heart* . . . / I bowed down toward thy holy temple / and give thanks to thy name for thy steadfast love and thy faithfulness" (Ps. 138:1-2).

Words and phrases from the Scriptures have a mysterious knack of finding expression in prayer. Often I have read a few verses, closed the Bible, and settled down to pray with someone, only to find that the things I read in the passage spring up in the words I say. While quotations from the Bible do not necessarily make our prayers more authentic, they can help us to discern how we should pray. Our prayers are fed by the Scriptures as we mentally digest what the Bible says and apply its teaching to what we ask God for.

Occasionally a text can speak prophetically or bring fresh hope to those who suffer. George Bennett described in *The Heart of Healing* (1971) how he was once asked to visit an old lady who was seriously ill. The doctor had warned her daughter that she was not likely to live for more than a day or two, and the daughter whispered this information to him as he went upstairs.

He sat by the old lady's bedside and, after a while, opened the Bible at John 14:1: "Let not your hearts be troubled; believe in God, believe also in me." As he read, the conviction came over him that the old lady was not going to die—at least, not in that illness—so when he had finished the passage, he said a prayer for healing.

Sure enough, she didn't die. She recovered to live happily for a further two years.

"The experience has always remained a mystery with me," he concluded, "but at the time I wondered if perhaps a power of healing had come into the life of the old lady during the reading of those lovely words."

2. A Spirit of Penitence

If the church's ministry to the sick in the past has sometimes been overloaded with a sense of guilt and a stress on sinfulness, that does not mean we can ignore the effects of sin when we pray for healing today. A lack of penitence, both in those who minister as well as in those to whom they minister, can block the flowing of God's grace. If those for whom we pray are not healed, then at least one question we can ask is: Has persistence in sin anything to do with it? There may be a lack of faith in the congregation, a disobedience to God in those who pray, and even a resentment or pride in those who are sick— innumerable combinations of individual and collective sin can stultify the healing ministry of a local church.

I have already discussed this in a previous chapter, but we still need to be reminded of it every time we pray with someone and every time someone prays with us. It was a factor behind one of the most remarkable healings I've ever known.

In my church a member of the congregation became chronically ill with a deteriorating disease in the upper part of her spine. Eileen was in and out of the hospital for weeks at a time. She was in constant pain; she had to wear a surgical collar. The crisis came when her surgeon said she ought to consider having an operation. This would, he said, halt the spread of the disease and relieve her pain; but he feared it would paralyze her from the waist downwards for the rest of her life.

She came regularly to the weekday services of prayer for healing in the church. For some years there was no obvious healing, but the deterioration in her spine was checked sufficiently for the surgeon to postpone the dreaded operation. Life was bearable but hardly ever free from pain. And she had one or two bouts in the hospital each year.

Later she visited a Christian community where she had long conversations with one of the members about her attitude towards her condition. When she returned home (she lived alone), she realized more clearly than before how bitter she had become about her troubles and how she had to repent and trust God for whatever her future might hold.

"Lord," she prayed, "if I have to go through life with all this pain, please take away my bitterness."

The church continued the services; and a few weeks after this prayer, Eileen had the laying on of hands with prayer in church. She felt a burning sensation at the back of her neck as they ministered to her. The pain continued for two or three days.

She was due to see the surgeon again the following week. What happened she described on a cassette she sent to me some weeks later:

"As the surgeon examined me, feeling each vertebra from the base of the spine upwards, I felt no pain, which was unusual. Usually when he touched certain vertebrae the pain was so great that I fainted.

"He seemed puzzled, and sent me for an X-ray, marking the note 'Urgent.' When the X-ray film came back, he looked at it for a long time, and then asked the orthopedic surgeon to come and see it as well. The orthopedic surgeon examined my spine thoroughly, then he looked again at the X-ray, and he seemed puzzled, too.

"They asked me what I had been doing that week. Very nervously, I said that I hadn't done anything, except that my pastor had anointed me for healing a few days previously. I told them how my neck had burned when he had laid hands on me, and you could see the looks of surprise on their faces. They had a quiet chat together, and when that was finished, they invited me to look at the X-ray plates they had been examining.

"On one plate, which had been taken three weeks ago, I could see the fibrous tissues blurring the image of the spine, but on the other plate—the one that had just been taken—the vertebrae stood out quite clearly.

'You can take your collar off,' they told me, 'and we'll trust you'll never have to wear it again. This is nothing less than a miracle.'"

Eileen left the hospital, slipped into a nearby church, and sobbed her thanksgiving to God. A blockage had been removed; a healing had been given. Since then she has been used in a worldwide ministry to bring encouragement and comfort to many sick people.

3. *The Community of God's People*

This ingredient doesn't mean that all prayers for the sick should be offered corporately or in the presence of other members of the church. Obviously such a restriction would be ridiculous. There may well be many occasions when we have to pray with the sick alone. What it does mean is that, when we pray with the sick, or when we are the subject of such prayer, we should be aware that the prayers are being offered in the body of Christ.

I'm not being theologically fastidious. All prayer, you say, is in union with Jesus Christ and with one another, so why mention it? For this reason: if we pray with a conscious awareness of the church, we shall be less likely to be diverted by our own ideas or idiosyncrasies and more flexible in the hands of God. When we think corporately we are less likely to act individualistically.

Praying with an awareness of the body of Christ has spin-offs in several directions in the ministry of healing.

It shows that those who are ministering are prepared to accept the oversight of the congregation's pastoral leadership. This is a guard against excesses and an opportunity for further help. The one who ministers does not then give the impression that he is the sole channel through which the charism of healing is to be expected. He prays knowing that others may have to be involved in the ministry, too, and that is a comfort to the one who listens to and joins in his prayer. Sometimes it may be necessary to refer certain distressed or sick individuals either to one with more experience or to qualified medical care. If we discern this as we pray with a sick person, our prayers will help them to prepare for and accept this further ministry.

It also helps the sick person to trust in what Jesus Christ can do through his body, the church, rather than through particular individuals. We are constantly tempted to rely on the woman or the man praying for us, whom we can see, rather than on the Lord, whom we cannot see. Our faith then starts swerving away from God to man. But this is not how the gifts of the Spirit operate. Individuals may be used extensively in the ministry of healing, but that doesn't make them healers in the true sense of the word. The Lord is our only healer, the church the covenanted channel of his grace—nothing less and nothing more.

When I spend an evening with a church group discussing the ministry of healing, I insist that I'm not there to lead them in that ministry but to encourage them to participate in it as members of Christ's body, as the Spirit leads them. If there is any ministering to do to individuals, I involve the group's leader and others with me in the prayer and the laying on of hands.

Some years ago I visited a church to lead such a group. Afterwards that congregation developed an extensive ministry to the sick, not unlike that in Faith Lutheran Church, Geneva, Illinois, described in the last chapter.

Recently I returned to that church to preach one Sunday. The pastor and one or two others were discussing their ministry when I happened to remark, "I never dreamed that little group I addressed would ever take you as far as this."

They looked at me in surprise.

"Did you—? Of course! We'd forgotten! You came to us years ago, didn't you?"

They were right to forget my earlier visit. Their ministry was the church's, not mine.

Services of prayer for healing, or a ministry of healing exercised in the context of a congregation's normal Sunday worship, serve to strengthen the truth that it is the church which is the minister—the church acting as the body of Christ. Other ministries of healing, by individuals or in groups, can then be related to these public acts of worship. It is a good pastoral strategy to involve in such services those who have taken a lead in the healing ministry in groups and elsewhere. I shall say more about this in the next chapter.

4. *Medical Opinion*

I've not met many modern Christians who hold to the old Pentecostal belief that only those who lack faith in God will go to see a doctor after they have received ministry for healing; but in our prayers for the sick we tend to ignore medical diagnosis and prognosis.

If we recognize that much medical care is a gift from God, then we should respect a doctor's opinion and skill in our petitions. We should ask the Holy Spirit to guide the patient's medical attendants and ask that healing may come through the care offered by doctors, nurses, and others. I've known one or two ministers who invoke God's blessing over the drugs (making the sign of the cross over the containers at the bedside!)

Relationships between the patient and those who care for him are obviously important. People who are sick at home or who are confined to the hospital sometimes find themselves at odds with their general practitioner or with the nurse in charge of the ward. Quite often the cause is trivial, but the aggravation which results can be distressing. This, too, should be a subject for prayer. What other steps are taken will depend on the circumstances. Is the complaint a minor affair, needing more toleration? Or is it serious enough to be investigated?

The doctor's report gives us a clue of what we should be praying about. It enables us to be specific. We can invoke the healing power of God on whatever has been diagnosed. Did the doctor say that the illness would take a certain course? Did he warn the patient that recovery would take a certain period of time? These facts we bring into our prayers, asking the Lord to carry the patient through the discomforts and setbacks to fullness of health.

Then we can ask God that the healing might be quicker than expected. It is not uncommon to find that, when the sick are prayed for in this way, the process of healing is speeded up. It is as if the various means of healing which come from God—loving support, medical and nursing care, prayer and sacrament—converge to accelerate the advent of his grace to that particular individual. Often, too, the unpleasant side effects of treatment fail to appear. For those who are beginners in the ministry of healing and hesitant about praying for the sick, this kind of intercession can be an early encouragement. They see positive results following from their ministry and their faith grows that God can do even greater works.

But what if the prognosis is grave? What if the doctor tells us that the patient is seriously ill?

It is not being disrespectful to medical opinion in these cases—or, indeed, in less serious cases—to pray for a miracle, if we believe that is what the Lord wants us to do. Scientific medicine approaches illness and disability through its own particular disciplines and, as we have seen, these do not take into account the possibility of a direct act of healing by God. Scientific medicine is a good deal more open to the unexpected now than it used to be, and I've never known Christian doctors with experience of the church's ministry of healing to be discouraging when I've suggested we pray that the Lord will overrule their opinions about a particular case. Indeed, if the cooperation between the church and the medical profession is developing locally along the lines described in the last chapter, the doctor may well be one of the ministering team.

I must confess, however, that I find it extremely difficult to offer advice on the question of when it is right to pray with the expectation that there will be a sudden, miraculous healing. I'm too conscious that anything I write will be either sadly misleading or totally inadequate. When we pray that God will act mightily among us, we face the mystery of his purposes and their fulfillment. That is holy ground on which we dare not tread. Certainly we should beware of anything that seems to tell the Lord what we think he ought to do.

I can only say that a Christian who is learning to walk in the Spirit as a disciple of Jesus Christ gradually develops an inner sense of what the Father's will is in the countless choices he has to make in daily life. He begins to know what the Father requires, just as Jesus knew in his ministry. This comes about because union with Christ enables the disciple to see things around him with his Master's eyes. Understanding God's word in the Scriptures, finding Christ in the fellowship of his body, the church, experiencing the Holy Spirit through living and learning with fellow Christians and others in the society to which he belongs—all these are used by God to reveal the path he is to take. We call this ability a gift of discernment—and it is one of the most important of all spiritual gifts, for it is the key to Christian obedience.

Of course, we're not infallible. The world, the flesh, and the devil challenge our obedience. The evil one strives to confuse or deceive us. We need to be humble and check what we believe may be God's will (say, in a prayer for healing) with the discernment and wisdom of others. Then out of such searching will come, from deep within ourselves, initiatives which we know are not ours. They are more central to our consciousness than our doubts and fears. It is these promptings which lead us to pray that God will heal the sick directly and unconditionally, even when the medical report is unhopeful.

The story I told in the first chapter illustrates how sometimes this prayer can lead us to the cross of Christ rather than to the immediate power of his resurrection as a sign of God's kingdom. But still the restoration of the church's ministry of healing means that our expectation of what God will do must be higher than our doubts and disappointments. We are to believe that God can do all that he has revealed in Jesus Christ, and we shall see his glory through what he does.

Occasionally both medical opinion and Christian discernment will tell us that a patient is terminally ill and that our prayer should not be for physical healing but for a peaceful death. Ministry to the dying is a precious service and requires far more space than I can give here. Various factors have to be taken into consideration. Has the patient been informed of his condition? Ought he to be told? What effect is the treatment he is receiving on his mental and emotional state? Is he a believer—or one who wants to believe? How are his family and friends reacting to the information?

Assuming the patient knows about his condition and is mentally alert to what is happening, we do not abandon hope that healing might come, but we recognize that it might be through death rather than through physical health. Our ministry to him in prayer will be as agents of God's love through whatever distress may assault him—periods of unbelief, fear, bitterness, depression. When he reaches the point where he can accept what is happening and reach out to the Lord, then our prayers move with him. If a medical opinion prepares us for that, then it is an integral part of the church's ministry of healing.

5. Thanksgiving and Praise

A devout Methodist I knew had a long illness which he bore with God's amazing grace. Supported by his wife and friends, he approached death serenely, his sufferings controlled by skillful medical care. A prayer group which he and his wife led used to meet in their house once a month, and throughout the husband's illness the group continued to assemble there, involving the sick man as much as possible.

When his condition became critical, the group suggested it meet elsewhere, but the man's wife wouldn't hear of it.

"We need your prayers more than ever now," she said.

So they had their meeting in her sitting room as usual. For part of the evening they went upstairs, stood round the bed, said a few prayers and softly sang several choruses. The sick man opened his eyes, smiled, and moved his lips as he faintly joined in. Then they tiptoed downstairs and the wife went into the kitchen to make coffee.

About ten minutes later, after she had passed the cups round, she went upstairs to see if her husband wanted anything. He was still smiling and looked peacefully asleep. It was some moments before she realized he was dead.

"It was a truly Christian passing," she said to me some weeks after the funeral. "He went to the Lord as he'd always wanted to—praising Jesus."

Experience shows that the sick receive all kinds of healing when they praise God—not just the healing of eternity, such as my friend received, but also physical and inner healings. It is a characteristic of praise that it turns us away from ourselves towards God. When we join in praise, we're not petitioning for ourselves, or interceding for another, or thinking about anyone else except the Lord. We are acknowledging him as our King, and in that acknowledgment he can do so much in us and through us.

Praise directs us towards obedience. Jesus glorified the Father during his earthly ministry, and Paul taught that we should praise God in all circumstances. Even in sickness we can, through praise, offer our diseased and painful bodies as "a living sacrifice, holy and acceptable to God, which is your spiritual worship" (Rom 12:1). We consciously surrender our body afresh to God with thanksgiving for the life he has given us. The therapeutic effect of this can be beneficial in itself, quite apart from any spiritual gift which may be manifested. My praise is my yes, my amen, to the Lord in the situation in which I find myself; it is my way of allowing him into every detail of my life, including my sickness, so that my life will be an alleluia of obedience to him.

That is why praise is such a powerful weapon in the struggle against evil. It banishes fear and self-pity; it turns indifference into zeal for God's service; it tears down the curtains of darkness and lets in the light and joy of God. "The joy of the Lord is your strength" (Neh 8:10).

Yet when we pray with the sick, we must be careful not to press them further into praise than they feel they are able to go. Praise can become a mockery rather than a prayer if a patient is surrounded by people singing choruses or offering thanks to God when he cannot sincerely make it his own. There is a delicate sensitivity in deciding when the sick need to be encouraged to praise and when prayer must meet them where they are.

In Devon, Pennsylvania, at the Regina Mundi Priory, there is a community of nuns known as the Sisters of Jesus Crucified. They are a community of disabled women—blind, deaf, crippled, chronically sick. Their motto is *Amen! Alleluia!* It sums up the spirit of their community: *Amen* reflects their acceptance of their condition and their determination not to give in to their conditions; *Alleluia* expresses their wholehearted response to him who works all things for the good of those who love him.

6. *Spiritual Gifts*

The basic charism in the church's ministry to the sick is the gift of healing; and in this ministry we can usually ask for that gift with reverence and hope. But in the course of exercising this ministry to individuals, other spiritual gifts may be manifested, and we have to be prepared for them. Discernment and testing are, of course, always necessary.

In the ministry itself the one who prays, or perhaps the one who is being prayed for, may be given a picture by the Holy Spirit which bears on the condition of the patient or on the probable outcome of the ministry. This picture is called "a simple vision." It is a vivid manner of revealing God's purposes and love.

I was once acting as the prayer partner to a woman as she ministered to a man, a doctor, who suffered from acute asthma. As we were laying hands on him, she was given a picture of a baby stifled in the tight clothes that an over-anxious mother had wrapped him in. She mentioned this, and it alerted the man to the tense relationship he had had with his mother and the way in which his asthma worsened when he had dealings with her. It was the beginning of his healing.

Some Christians have charisms which enable them to minister to certain kinds of cases better than others. It is almost as if God equips them to be "specialists." Christians who have experienced and been healed of a sickness are often able to assist others with the same trouble; but the principle of specialization goes further than simply sharing in common experiences. Some seem to be used in praying with cancer victims, others with those suffering from skin diseases, and so on.

Certain manifestations can be alarming if they are not expected. As the ministry of healing is being restored in the churches during the current spiritual renewal, unfamiliar practices and experiences have emerged among some groups and congregations. One of these, variously called "being slain in the Spirit" or "resting in the Spirit," is when the person receiving prayer with the laying on of hands appears to lose consciousness, slumping to the floor from a chair or from a standing position. Another is a violent spasm of weeping, often with loud cries which echo round the building.

The fact that such practices and experiences are unfamiliar in the churches does not mean that they have no value. On the contrary, some of those who have been "slain in the Spirit" or caught up in a spasm of uncontrollable weeping have later declared that the experience was a key factor in their healing—the former as a kind of divine anaesthetic, the latter as a means of deep release. But it is an area where autosuggestion can be let loose, and it needs careful discernment and firm handling. The criterion is the same for these as for any other manifestation purporting to be a spiritual gift: does it glorify Jesus Christ, does it build up his church, does it promote the fruit of the Spirit among God's people—particularly love?

This is where ministering in teams or groups provides added strength. Again and again Christians working together have noticed how the Holy Spirit distributes his gifts enabling individuals to support and supplement each other's ministries, so that the total ministry of the team or group is much greater than the sum of their individual charisms.

For four years in the 1970s I was a member of a fellowship where about a dozen of us lived, prayed, and worked together as a community ministering to the many people who came to our week or weekend conferences. We saw how individuals or couples facing particular difficulties seemed to be led by God to certain members of the community who had gifts for helping people in those areas.

Those who receive healing can also receive new gifts for reaching out to others. It is a sign that the Lord has raised them up from their illness, not just to enjoy a healthier life but also to be enabled to serve him further than was possible before they were ill. Jesus sent the sick he healed away with encouragement to thank and worship his heavenly Father. He still does this through the healing ministry of his church.

7. Expectant Faith

I've left this to the end of the list because it stands by itself. Expectant faith permeates all the other ingredients. Whatever we discern through the others, it is faith which makes our participation in prayer for healing real.

Let me put it this way. The ingredients of prayer which I have just listed are like the colors used for a painting. They are laid out one by one ready for use when required. But they remain in the box until we take the brush and apply the paints to the paper. So it is with faith: it is like the brush. The other ingredients become effective because, as we refer to them for guidance in our prayer, there is an underlying movement of faith in God through Jesus Christ.

Misunderstandings arise when faith is discussed in relationship to healing. This is because the word has been carelessly used. Think how the term "faith healing" is still attached to almost any non-medical aid offered to the sick. So often it implies nothing more than faith in the ability of another human being (or, worse still, faith in spiritual powers which are inherently evil).

Of course, in all forms of medical care we have to *trust* people. We trust the surgeon when we sign the form giving permission for him to operate on our bodies. We say we have faith in our doctor—meaning the same thing. But faith in God is very different. Indeed, faith in God is better expressed as faith *into* Christ—that is, throwing ourselves forward into his care and under his Lordship for everything in our lives, past, present, and future.

One great stumbling block to expectant faith is not so much unbelief as fear: fear of being made a fool of, fear of hurting someone, fear of misinterpreting the guidance of the Holy Spirit. Suppose nothing happens when we've prayed for healing? What effect will that have on the person we've prayed for? How can we be sure we're praying for the right thing?

The best answer to fear is to have a firm grasp of what it means to be accepted by God. He sees us "in Christ." It's a status he's given us, not because we deserve it but because Christ deserves it for us. We can rely totally on him because we know that we are totally acceptable to him, provided we are wanting to follow Jesus and are trying to obey him.

And then, because he has accepted us in his love, we can reach out to help others in love, too. We don't want to mislead or falsely encourage the people we minister to, but there will be occasions when what we hope and pray for doesn't come about as we expected it would. Yes, there will be disappointments. But if we have made it our primary aim to love those we minister to, we shall find that they're not as hurt by these disappointments as we might expect them to be. They will know that we care about them—and that can be a healing gift which is very precious to them (which is why pastoral care must always be associated with sacramental signs and charismatic power in this ministry).

I grow uneasy when I hear some teacher urging those who need healing to believe in the promises of God and to accept their healing from him by faith even when the symptoms have not begun to disappear. This seems to me to impose an intolerable strain on those who cannot achieve such a degree of certainty. If we argue that God always does heal physically when asked to do so, provided we have faith, then there's only one person to blame if we pray in that way and find we're not healed—ourselves. We're forced to conclude that we didn't have enough faith and that we're still saddled with the consequences.

Such teachers also tell us that we should not use qualifying phrases when we pray for healing. To add words like, "if it be your will, Lord," to a prayer, they say, is an indication that we don't have faith in the Spirit's guidance. We're not really believing God will heal. And, again, I grow uneasy when I hear this. Jesus himself qualified the most intense prayer he ever offered ("My Father, if it be possible, let this cup pass from me" [Mt 26:39]. Surely if we're not always sure how to pray, it's better to be honest and say so.)

Faith isn't a matter of working up feelings of confidence in God, rather as if we're warming up a car engine on a cold morning. We're called to believe *in God*—not to have faith in our faith! I begin to crumple when I think of faith as a personal quality. I only begin to feel secure when I put my trust in what God wants and in what he can do. It's not my words that count (qualifications or not); it's my obedience to him. "Yet not as I will, but as you will," Jesus concluded his prayer. The results can be left in God's hands.

Of course, if we don't have enough faith in God to pray in obedience to him in every situation—and all the Christians I've ever met have started from that point and often returned to it again and again—then we need to confess our unbelief and ask him to renew us in faith.

One of the mysteries of faith is that, although it constitutes our deepest response to God for what he has done for us in Jesus Christ, yet it is at the same time a gift from him when we lift our eyes beyond ourselves. He meets us with faith when we want to have faith. Sometimes faith comes when we want to love him because he first loved us. Sometimes it comes when we begin to hope in him. Faith, hope, and love intertwine with one another as we long to be able to give ourselves to the Lord, especially in prayer for the sick. That is why our prayer is expectant—hopeful.

Yet, when all this has been said, faith isn't an essential condition for the gift of healing. It was not always apparent in those who came to Jesus and the apostles. God doesn't strike a bargain with us: "I'll heal you if you have enough faith." That is why it sometimes happens that individuals with very little faith are sometimes miraculously healed while committed Christians remain in their sickness.

I have been prayed for with expectant faith and yet not been healed for a long time; I have been prayed for without any conscious faith on my part and been healed.

A few years ago I had a painful attack of shingles up one side of my body. The doctor's prescription was rest during the day and distalgesic for night time. Both sitting and lying down were equally uncomfortable.

I canceled all my engagements for the next two weeks except one. The engagement I didn't cancel was an address I was due to give to a group of clergy. I went to the meeting and spoke from a cushioned armchair.

At the end of the meeting some of the others came to lay hands on me and to pray for healing. I accepted their ministrations gratefully, but the possibility that I might be healed through them never entered my head. Yet within twenty-four hours the soreness and the marks on my skin had vanished, and they have never returned.

The incident reminded me yet again that in all questions about the ministry of healing we are driven back to the mystery of God's sovereignty.

Belief in God's sovereignty is another way of saying we believe in the kingdom of God. When we pray with attention to the Scriptures, in a spirit of penitence and humility, within the community of God's people, with respect for medical opinion, in thanksgiving and praise, and with discernment of spiritual gifts, our ministry is revealed to us within the perspective of God's kingdom.

That kingdom may be manifested now in signs such as gifts of healing, but it is also a kingdom which is to come. That is what theologians call its eschatological dimension—seeing the kingdom in the light of God's final purposes. In that dimension we see that perfect health for women and men is his will, but that any healing in this world can only be provisional. Disease and death will not finally be destroyed until the perfect reign of God in the age which is to come. We live in the in-between time, after the ascension of Christ and before his second coming.

Because the kingdom of God has not yet been fully revealed, we cannot say that every prayer for healing will be effective in curing every disease or in postponing death. Healing is one of the most striking manifestations of the redemption of our bodies which salvation will bring; but it is an anticipation graciously and mysteriously vouchsafed to some and, equally graciously and mysteriously, withheld from others. Complete wholeness of body, mind, and spirit belongs to eternity; the prayer of faith acknowledges that.

TEN

A Being-Healed
Community

W E HAVE SEEN HOW SPIRITUAL RENEWALS set in motion movements to restore to the church her ministry of healing at the beginning of this century. We have also seen how in recent decades new Pentecostals have been influential in bringing together the pastoral, sacramental, and charismatic elements of this ministry into a New Testament pattern.

Now observers of the worldwide church have detected a "third wave" of spiritual renewal which is taking the ministry of healing into a field far wider than that occupied by new Pentecostals. The name, the Third Wave, owes its origin to the somewhat limited view that classic Pentecostalism represented the "first wave" and new Pentecostalism the "second wave." The Third Wave consists of the increasing number of Christians who reject the philosophical materialism which has dominated theology for so long and who believe that God can and does intervene in our lives. More and more Episcopalians, Anglicans, Lutherans, Reformed, Methodists, and Baptists, as well as Roman Catholics, are returning to a faith that God still reveals himself through our experience of his word and power. So to them it is no longer unscientific to expect God to act beyond what is known through medical research and practice. Like new Pentecostals they also look for miraculous healings.

143

Consequently there is throughout the Christian world today a growing conviction that every local church is called to minister healing. It is the result of a fresh realization of what it means to be a fellowship of the Holy Spirit, and of a new understanding of Paul's question, "Do all possess gifts of healing?" (1 Cor 12:30).

A generation ago many scholars would have argued that since the Greek version of the text makes it clear the apostle was expecting a negative answer, he was not looking for a ministry of healing everywhere. Nowadays we interpret him differently. We have come to appreciate that the church is a charismatic community in which different members exercise different ministries, and that this was the point of Paul's rhetorical question. He was emphasizing that different ministries must be exercised in harmony with one another—including the ministry of healing—*within the one congregation.* He would have been horrified if his question had been taken to mean that some congregations had *no* ministry of healing. He had explained earlier in the letter that God bestows his spiritual gifts as they are needed for the building up of the church, and he would certainly have added—if the matter had been put to him—that every congregation needs charisms of healing to fulfill its corporate ministry.

The church has never singled out "healers" as members with a special ministry as it has singled out apostles, bishops, presbyters, evangelists, and deacons. Nowhere in the Bible is the title of healer used except of God (Ex 15:26). Individuals have occasionally been commissioned to exercise a healing ministry, but this simply meant that they were recognized as being able to give a lead to the rest of us.

In a local church there may well be two or three members who are used more than others by God in a ministry of healing—or in a certain aspect of it, such as counseling and inner healing. If so, then they should be supported by the congregation and offered opportunities of further training and experience. But we should beware of calling them "healers." There is no scriptural justification for the label, and Christian tradition has honored that limitation.

My impression is that in the ministry of healing almost anyone in a congregation may be involved at some time or other. Hence we should expect each local church to exercise these gifts as it does other ministries, such as pastoral leadership, preaching, teaching, evangelism, hospitality, administering the accounts, and so on. The way in which the ministry is fulfilled will vary according to circumstances. What is customary in a West Indian Pentecostal congregation may not be appropriate in a middle-class Methodist suburban congregation (though they might learn much from one another).

We find this ministry developing at different levels in a local church—in the home, in a group, in a special service, as well as within the Sunday liturgy.

A Domestic Ministry

Parents lay hands on their sick children, members of families pray for one another, friends minister to friends. And many experience the healing of Christ in their midst. If the stories of these countless domestic miracles could be collected and published, what a library would be assembled!

Most of those who pray for one another at home in this way are probably not conscious that they are engaging in something called "the church's ministry of healing." They just regard themselves as Christians who are responding to sickness in a Christian manner. Yet in so ministering, they are acting as a cell of the body of Christ. The Christian family has been called "a little church." Where two or three are gathered together in Christ's name, there we have the smallest unit for the church's ministry.

And healings that happen in the home can have a widespread influence.

The mother of an eleven-year-old girl noticed that her daughter was going bald on the crown of her head. She took the girl to the doctor, who referred the case to the local hospital. The treatment which the girl received had no effect. Her hair continued to fall out. Eventually the mother was advised that her daughter would have to attend a special clinic in a city some miles away, but was warned that it would take some months before an appointment could be arranged.

The mother remembered a sermon she had heard about praying for the sick, and so at every bedtime she placed her hands on her daughter's head and asked the Lord to make the hair grow again. Within quite a short period she was thrilled to see wisps of hair appear on the bald patch. Soon she was able to cancel the arrangements to visit the special clinic.

This mother told me her story one Saturday when I was at a teaching weekend at the church she attended. On the following day, as I was standing at the back of the church before the Sunday morning service began, I saw her come in accompanied by a girl. The latter had a mass of beautiful auburn hair falling over her shoulders. The mother saw me looking at her daughter, and she smiled and nodded.

At the evening service (the daughter being at home) I persuaded the mother to give a short testimony about the healing. She had never spoken in public before, but what she said was far more effective than all the addresses I had given that weekend. The ministry of healing was not something talked about by a visiting clergyman any more: it was happening in the midst of that congregation!

A Group Ministry

Initiatives in the ministry of healing are often made in small groups. Among six or eight people it is easier to take risks of faith in praying for one another. You feel you know one another well enough to make mistakes!

My own attitude towards this ministry was affected by an experience I had in a group quite a few years ago. We had met over a number of months to read the Bible together, to listen to tapes, and to discuss and pray about spiritual renewal.

One evening I went to the group with a terrible cold. I should have stayed away to avoid spreading the infection, but the group was at an interesting stage in its discussions and I didn't want to miss it. Somehow I struggled through the Bible reading and the talk that followed. Halfway through the prayers, one of the group got up and, without any prompting from me, came behind my chair and prayed for my healing with the laying on of hands. Next morning when I got up all traces of the cold had vanished—an unusual occurrence, since those infections generally hang around me for a week or more.

The incident was influential for three reasons. It was the first time in my life that I had ever had hands laid on me for healing. It was the first time I experienced healing directly as a result of prayer. And it was a cultural if not a theological shock to a clergyman like myself in those days to receive such a ministry from a woman!

Prayer for healing in groups is widespread throughout the denominations. It occurs principally in groups which have come together through the impulse of the new Pentecostal movement. In some, such prayer is offered only when the need arises; in others, members are led to specialize in this ministry and to contribute to its development within the life of the parent congregation.

The relationship between the group and the parent congregation is all-important in this ministry, as it is when groups become established for any reason. Ministries of healing and deliverance in groups can go wrong if the group is not submitted to the pastoral leadership of the local church. Because small groups can be powerful cells of Christian presence, they are also vulnerable to satanic attacks.

One scenario for disaster is where the pastor of the local church has theological difficulties about the ministry of healing and fears about the possible outcome of it. This leads him to distance himself from the group, thus causing the group to feel he doesn't trust them or care about them. Another scenario is where, after one or two remarkable healings in answer to prayer, the members of the group begin to think of themselves more highly than they ought to think and dismiss the pastor and the rest of the congregation as "un-spiritual" or "uncharismatic."

The ingredients in prayer for healing listed in the previous chapter are particularly relevant for groups if their ministry to the sick is to be fruitful for the kingdom of God rather than divisive in the local church. For almost all development in the ministry of healing in local churches that I know of has been initiated by a few who met together to study the subject and to pray about it in small groups. Leaders of congregations and leaders of groups must keep in touch with one another if this is to happen.

A Congregational Ministry

Services of prayer for healing in the congregation have become popular in recent years. They demonstrate publicly that the local church is concerned with healing and they bear witness to the power of the gospel in a striking way. On several occasions I have taken part in missions in a neighborhood which began with such a service. Each time testimonies to the healing grace of God had a penetrating effect in bringing home the truth that Jesus Christ came to save us.

The form of these services varies, but the following model is satisfactory for both large and small congregations:

A Service of Prayer for Healing

Introduction
    Hymn
    Announcement
    Preparatory prayer
Ministry of the Word of God
    Scripture reading
    Hymn, psalm, canticle, or song
    Scripture reading
    Sermon and/or testimony
Ministry of Prayer for Healing
    General confession and absolution
    Affirmation of faith
    Intercessions
    Laying on of hands (and anointing)
    Act of praise and thanksgiving
    Dismissal

Other hymns, songs, solo items, and so on, are included as appropriate.

This model has a traditional liturgical shape—a ministry of the Word of God followed by a response in which prayer for healing is central.

The *Introduction* provides material for the congregation to affirm before God why they have come together. The announcement, given early in the proceedings, prepares everyone, especially those who are seeking personal ministry, for what is going to take place. The preparatory prayer asks God to send the Holy Spirit to guide and equip everyone for this ministry.

The *Ministry of the Word of God* helps the congregation to look expectantly at the Lord and to listen to what he has to say to them. The passages of Scripture are read in a manner that aids reflection; the hymn, psalm, canticle, or song draws out the meaning of the passages and enables the congregation to respond to what they hear;

the address underlines the teaching of the Scriptures. A testimony from someone who has recently experienced healing can often be a very effective illustration to the theme of the address.

The *Ministry of Prayer* moves through the various ingredients needed in prayer as the local congregation presents its needs before God. The general confession and absolution asks the Lord to remove the barrier of sin. The affirmation of faith (perhaps made in the form of the baptism interrogations, e.g., "Do you believe in God the Father . . . in his Son Jesus Christ . . . in the Holy Spirit . . . ?") enables the congregation to build one another up, especially those going forward for the laying on of hands. During the intercessions individual members of the congregation can call out the names of people they know who are ill.

Prayer with the laying on of hands (and perhaps anointing as well) is the climax of the service. Those requiring ministry go forward, in some churches with a friend or prayer partner, or raise their hands if it is not convenient to leave their seats.

Experience shows whether it is better for the congregation to sing quietly during the time of ministry, or to pray silently for those being ministered to.

Since, as we have seen it is nearly always better for the praying and the laying on of hands to be done by two rather than by one, there must be in a congregation a sufficient number of people who have been trained for this. Those who have experienced this ministry in groups can often be invited to help, thus creating a link between the on-going ministry of healing in the groups and that in their local congregation.

If olive oil is used, the leader of the ministering team dips his or her thumb in the oil and makes the sign of the cross on the forehead with words such as, "I anoint you in the name of the Father and of the Son and of the Holy Spirit." Other prayers, of course, can be added. It is handy to have a piece of cotton wool available to wipe off excess oil.

Should anointing always be used with the laying on of hands when ministering to the sick?

I don't know any set answer to that question, but we need to be careful in our use of sacramental signs. The indiscriminate use of infant baptism, for example, has made that particular sign a matter of grave division among Christians. The laying on of hands is a sign which can accompany any prayer for healing and strengthening, even for comparatively minor ailments; but anointing should be reserved for critical moments—when an illness is first diagnosed, before an operation, at the end of a session in which the first fruits of inner healing are apparent, and so on. When anointing someone regularly, I have usually done so every one or two months, unless they were dangerously ill, in which case I administered the oil more frequently. As with all sacramental signs, the one who administers and the one who receives should prepare in an appropriate manner.

When the news of a service of prayer for healing gets around a neighborhood, it sometimes attracts people to it who do not normally come to church. A congregation has a responsibility towards such people who come for help—to teach them about the saving work of Jesus Christ as well as to assist them in practical needs. There is something incomplete in a ministry of healing which offers only sacramental and charismatic means of grace and not pastoral care as well.

A Ministry within the Sunday Liturgy

Once the members of a congregation have become familiar with the ministry of healing through services like these, they begin to seek prayer for healing on other occasions—especially during the church services on Sundays. They argue, quite reasonably, that if they require prayer for healing they don't need to wait until the next special service is due. Hence the custom is spreading of prayer for healing for individuals within the context of the Sunday liturgy.

There is much to be said for this (provided it is well organized and doesn't keep the rest of the congregation in their pews for an inordinate length of time). All worship, especially communion and eucharist, is a coming together of God's people to receive—among other things—his healing grace. So prayer with the laying on of hands draws out for the individuals who present themselves what is already within the liturgy.

In the communion (taking this as the central act of worship) Jesus Christ is present in the assembled congregation who have come together in his name. He is present also in the ministry of the Word and in the sacramental signs of bread and wine. His presence brings salvation, of which healing is a sign. When we pray for salvation in the liturgy, then, we are also praying for healing.

Worship in itself gives us healing graces. The ministry of the Word invites us to put our trust in God. Many Bible readings underline this. "Fear not, little flock, for it is your Father's good pleasure to give you the kingdom" (Lk 12:32). And when so much illness has its roots in anxiety, the Scriptures provide us with the antidote: faith in God. "There is no fear in love, but perfect love casts out fear" (1 Jn 4:18). Again and again in its formal prayers the liturgy assures us that the kingdom of God is ours if we trust him and open ourselves to his Holy Spirit.

Through the ministry of the word and through the prayers God constantly invites us to cast all our cares on him. He is our rock, our shield, our stronghold, our deliverer—the images pile up to encourage us to cooperate with him. We are urged to take the risk of surrendering our anxieties, our illnesses, our lives, to him for complete healing. When Jesus met the sick man by the pool, he asked him, "Do you want to be healed?" (Jn 5:6). So, too, he asks us, "Do you want to be healed?" The liturgy helps us to answer, "Yes, Lord, by your grace!"

Expressions of penitence and general confessions enable us to seek God's forgiveness. One form reads:

You were sent to heal the contrite: Lord, have mercy.

The prayer of absolution affirms the Lord's willingness to receive those who turn to him in repentance. Prayers, songs, psalms, and canticles of praise give us an opportunity to reach out in thanksgiving to God for what he has already done to heal us and for what he is going to do.

Then there is Christ's healing presence in the sacramental signs of bread and wine. Whatever theological controversies may have surrounded the Church's eucharistic doctrines, it is the universal Christian belief that through his sacrifice on the cross and his resurrection, Jesus is present as host at his supper and that through the gift of the Holy Spirit he offers himself to his disciples as spiritual food.

And there is healing in the company of our fellow worshipers. The love of the Christian community brings great comfort and restores our sense of well-being. The widespread practice of the giving of the peace demonstrates our unity in the Spirit. "The peace of the Lord be with you," we say to one another, as we shake hands as a sign of mutual acceptance. "You are no longer strangers and sojourners, but you are fellow citizens with the saints and members of the household of God" (Eph 2:19). Whatever factors loneliness might contribute to illness, these should be dispelled if a congregation is as caring as the giving of the peace symbolizes.

Many of the sick are, of course, unable to get to church and have to be ministered to in their own homes or in the hospital. The custom of taking the reserved sacrament to the sick, or celebrating the eucharist in their homes, is as old as the church herself. Where only the pastor and the sick person are present, however, something of the corporate nature of celebration is lacking, and often arrangements are made for one or two others from the congregation to be there, too.

In recent years a number of Roman Catholic churches have developed a "communion by extension" through the use of lay ministers of the eucharist. After training and commissioning, lay men and women take the consecrated bread and wine from the altar at Sunday mass and, with one or two companions, visit the sick in their own homes to give them communion. They hold short services at the bedside and often pray with the laying on of hands as well. It is a powerful expression of the church's pastoral, sacramental, and charismatic ministry to the sick within a parochial framework.

One of the prayers used on these occasions sums it up well:

> Lord, through this sacrament
> may we rejoice in your healing power,
> and experience your love in mind and body.

The question is often raised: Should we expect special services of prayer for healing to be dropped from the program of a local church once that ministry is established in house groups and in the ordinary Sunday liturgy?

I don't think there is a set program for this ministry. We need to be flexible so that we can minister in the power of the Holy Spirit to human need wherever we encounter it. As long as there is illness of any kind, prayer for healing will always be necessary, especially in our homes and in our groups. Special services may well continue to serve a useful purpose even when the healing ministry is offered during the Sunday liturgy, especially when linked with the on-going teaching and outreach of a congregation. On the other hand, some sick folk prefer to be ministered to privately in their own homes or in a group, and their preferences should be respected.

What will always be necessary, whatever the program a local church adopts for its ministry of healing, will be the undergirding of teaching and prayer by its members. Otherwise the ministry will degenerate into just another stunt to impress adherents and to attract attention. That temptation was overthrown when it presented itself to Jesus Christ in the wilderness; and we must turn our backs on the same temptation, too.

A Healing Community?

In the last few pages of this book I want to suggest how we can participate in the ministry of healing as it is being restored in the church today. We can do this as individual Christians and as members of local congregations.

But before I spell out four guidelines, I must emphasize that first and foremost we can only participate by being willing to yield ourselves more and more to the Holy Spirit ourselves, as individuals and as congregations. Whether we are helped by one of the current movements of spiritual renewal—new Pentecostalism, the Third Wave, or whatever—is a secondary matter. It's our personal relationship with the Lord which is fundamental.

That is why there is no technique for introducing the ministry of healing to a local church. It's not like getting worshipers to accept a new hymn book. The ministry of healing is already there in the congregation if the Lord is present with them. The ministry is activated as they begin to be more faithful and more prayerful, believing that God can and will use them in Jesus Christ's saving work through the power of the Holy Spirit.

Having said that, however, there are certain practical things we can do.

1. Every Christian should learn how she or he can exercise this ministry personally when led by the Holy Spirit to do so.

Just as every responsible human being should know a few basic facts about first aid in case of emergency, so every Christian should know how to pray with someone when they are sick or in distress.

That may seem obvious, but in fact a large number of church folk are very hesitant about praying with others. They feel inadequate about it; they are doubtful about the reaction of those they pray with. Some in traditionally hierarchical denominations believe that such a ministry is the special job of the ordained clergy.

We have seen that, although certain individuals in the church are often used in this ministry more frequently than others, praying for the sick is not reserved for the few. Anyone who prays can pray for another. Whether or not gifts of healing follow our prayer is God's business. It may not always be possible or desirable to lay hands on those we pray for. It is sufficient that we respond faithfully to the inner prompting that we should pray for the sick person we are visiting or for the individual who has just confided in us about a personal distress.

Guidance about whether or not they would welcome such a ministry can often come in the answer to the simple question, "Would you like me to pray with you?" If the other seems uncomfortable, it will probably be right not to pursue the matter further just then. But if the answer is "Yes, please," then we can take the other's hand, turn our attention to God, and trust his Spirit to give us the words we are to use in the prayer.

Pastors of congregations have a particular responsibility to ensure that their members can pray in this way for others; that entails training, which leads me on to my next suggestion.

2. *Every local church should review regularly its participation in the ministry of healing through pastoral care, sacramental signs, and charismatic power.*

Under its leaders congregations should ask: How do we really cope with the illnesses and weakness among our fellowship and among those we are in contact with in the neighborhood? Are we using all the resources for healing which the Lord offers us in pastoral care, sacramental signs, and charismatic power? Is the ministry of healing an important focus in our praying, teaching, and decision-making?

A local church should be a fellowship in which members are encouraged to adopt healthy lifestyles—in rejecting those pressures and habits which increase strain and sickness, and in promoting those which build up healthy people and harmonious relationships. A disciplined life is the basis for any healthful program for women and men, and forgiveness and acceptance is the foundation of trusting relationships anywhere. If the gospel is, as we believe it to be, the means *par excellence* to healing and health, then the local church should reflect that. There is something sadly wrong with a congregation if its members are quarrelsome and ridden by neuroses year after year. The healthfulness of a congregation is assessed by how far the fruit of the Spirit is experienced among its members.

Consistent training is vital—what the Bible teaches about healing, how the ministry of healing is developing in the contemporary church, and what medical science can show us that is relevant to it. If this training is not to be merely an intellectual exercise, it will entail involving the members of the congregation in places where they can experience that ministry and be encouraged to participate in it themselves.

It has puzzled me for a long time why the educational agencies of the denominations have neglected to provide back-up for teaching about the ministry of healing. They spend much time and cash on training for stewardship schemes and projects on this or the latest ecumenical document, but I hardly ever hear of programs launched by dioceses, districts or provinces to help local churches become centers for healing. It is nearly always left to individuals and groups to take initiatives for the rest of us outside the denominational structures.

One consequence is the appearance of itinerant teachers with their teams. They travel from city to city, town to town, usually with a personal emphasis that characterizes their message (discerning of spirits, inner healing, power evangelism, and so on). They have a useful role in shaking up congregations and making them more aware of what the Lord wants them to do. But we should beware of accepting everyone. All kinds of people are scrambling on to this bandwagon as interest in the ministry of healing grows and as the denominations fail to provide teaching within their structures. Newsletters, computerized address lists, cassettes, videos, teaching notes, and books flow out from the headquarters of the itinerants in North America, Western Europe, and other countries. Television programs are produced. The focus is often on a big name. A good question to ask any teacher is: Are you answerable to a Christian community which itself submits to the authority of the wider church?

Yet there is also spreading a more local and mutual encouragement of this ministry. Members of one congregation visit another to share in what they have experienced of God's healing grace. Visits take place across denominational boundaries as well as within them. Usually this is preferable to the itinerant preacher with his amazing stories and spectacular presentations. The host congregation can identify itself more easily with a group from another local church. The opportunity to undertake such a visit is a great spur to training among the members of the visiting group.

When a congregation becomes aware of its ministry to the sick, it has a powerful incentive to pray. More than almost any other topic, the needs of the sick drive people to their knees. It is so worthwhile—especially when the gifts of healing appear! And this, in its turn, can be a means of leading congregations into other forms of Christian devotion.

The organization of the ministry of healing in a local church requires discernment and discipline.

Discernment is the gift of seeing where the Lord wants us to go. It also enables us to reject leadings by others who are not in his will. It is a charism which enables individuals, groups, and whole congregations to respond to the promptings of the Holy Spirit when they are confronted with human need—especially, in this case, sickness in all its complexities.

Discipline is the art of responding to the Holy Spirit within the unity which Jesus Christ gives to those he calls. It is the working out of our obedience to him within the church, under its leadership and in its corporate life.

When held together in love, discernment and discipline enable the local church to minister to the sick in such a way that their ministry becomes a manifestation of the Lord's own ministry as he exercised it himself in the days of his flesh.

3. Every local church should seek to cooperate with secular health services and other agencies in the neighborhood which care for people in sickness and trouble of all kinds.

Many of these services and agencies have taken their inspiration, as we have seen, from the church's pastoral care of the sick in the past. Although some of the things they offer are not acts of healing in the Christian understanding of God's purposes (e.g., abortion on demand), much that they do is a sign of the healing Christ who identified himself with human need: "As you did it to one of the least of these my brethren, you did it to me" (Mt 25:40).

Most congregations have some members who actually work professionally or voluntarily in hospitals and other centers. We can ask their advice about the local church's support for their work. What kind of back-up would they welcome from the rest of the congregation? What are they able to share with us that will help us to discern more clearly what our role should be as a Christian community in the neighborhood? Other members can be encouraged to offer themselves for care schemes or to take the initiative in setting up new projects when they are required.

Often it is good to join with other local churches in an ecumenical ministry for this task. Members of one tradition usually find their denominational differences shrinking in significance as they come together to serve the Lord in the society in which they live.

Cooperation with secular health services and other agencies must be undertaken humbly. We should not, as a local church, go to them as if we were experts just because we have experienced two or three miraculous healings in our Sunday worship over the last few months! Even if we believe the Christian ministry of healing contains what is essential to bring women and men to wholeness and salvation, there is still much that these services and agencies can teach us.

The church generally is fond nowadays of regarding herself as "a healing community." It is the title of many sermons and articles and of one or two books. Yet the outsider, looking at the church with her obvious weaknesses and divisions, might well say to her, "Physician, heal thyself!"

That is why I prefer the clumsier title I've chosen for this chapter: "a being-healed community." For it is only when we, as an assembly of Christians, continue to acknowledge our own need for healing in its fullest sense that we can, in our turn, become means of showing others where God's healing grace is to be found. It is another version of the old adage that the difference between a Christian and a non-Christian is that the former can tell the latter where they can both find bread.

4. Every local church should relate its ministry of healing to its mission as a community anointed by the Holy Spirit to live and proclaim the gospel of the kingdom of God in society today.

The being-healed community does not just set its sights on the healing of the sick within and outside its fellowship. It sees that ministry in the light of the salvation which came into the world through Jesus Christ. That involves suffering and sacrifices as well as healings and victories.

Local churches are called to challenge those policies and activities which spread so much ill health in our society—the things which break up families and rob individuals of their basic human rights, which undermine social and racial harmony, and which crush the poor and the powerless.

Because healing is a sign of the kingdom, then the local church which exercises a ministry of healing must also set the principles of the kingdom against everything which influences how we live. Often it will mean demonstrating through the quality of the Christian community's life that those who follow Jesus Christ have to turn upside down many of the ambitions and attitudes which women and men accept as normal. Often it will mean taking action to exorcise the evil which the Holy Spirit reveals to us in the society in which we live. If we are to be a being-healed community, we have to be involved socially to bring healing to others and to deliver them from the evil one.

Then the local church is in an authentic position to proclaim the gospel of the kingdom. The healings of Christ accompanied and manifested the good news of the salvation he announced in the power of the Spirit; similarly the church's announcement of the same good news can be accompanied and manifested in healing and deliverances. While I do not relish the phrase "signs and wonders evangelism," I recognize that local churches in many parts of the world have long neglected the ministry of healing as a component of their mission.

There are no blueprints for this to which the local church can turn. Our task is to discern and share in the healing ministry of Jesus Christ as he leads us in today's world. I have tried to show how his example can be analyzed in terms of pastoral care, sacramental signs, and charismatic power, and how these aspects of his ministry are unfolding in the church. For all of us, there is so much more that can be done in his name.

But it will mean facing the tragedies as well as the joys, the suffering of the cross as well as the healing of the diseased. When our prayers for healing do not seem to be answered, we shall encounter the crucified Lord. When we reach out to help those ensnared in spiritual sickness, we shall do battle with the devil.

While I have been writing this book, my mind has gone back to the story of Heather which I told at the beginning. Her words have often come back to me:

"I'm ready to go to the Lord, if he wants me to. I'm giving myself to him each day. But—I pray he may spare me long enough for me to see my little boys grow up . . ."

We shall find personal Gethsemanes as well as Galilean miracles in the ministry of healing; and that is something both we and the members of our local churches have to be prepared for.

Yet there will be healings, too—healings which give glory to God and which equip people for the service of his kingdom here and now.

Let me end this book with another story:

One day, in the early 1970s, I was being driven through the Irish countryside to address a meeting of new Pentecostals. It was late in the afternoon, when Cecil, my host and driver, noticed that the road was leading us close to where a friend of his, a bishop of the Church of Ireland, lived.

"John Armstrong's been ill," he said, "Let's go pray with him."

Within a few minutes he had parked the car outside his friend's house and we were being shown into the living room. John sat in a chair by the fire with a traveling rug over his knees. He apologized for remaining seated. He had, he told us, become partially paralyzed in the lower part of his body and he could only walk with the aid of crutches.

We chatted for a while as his wife brought in tea. Then, before we said goodbye, Cecil and I prayed with him, standing by his chair and laying hands on his head.

Years later, he described what had happened later that evening.

He had gone to bed early, aided by his wife, but had woken up just before midnight. He had got out of bed, gone into the bathroom, and returned. Just as he was settling down to sleep once more, he realized with a shock that he had not used his crutches. Slowly he got out of bed again and took a few steps. Yes, he really was better! Although his legs were stiff, he could walk without **his** crutches for the first time for months. He was so excited he woke his wife up to show her. Within a few days the paralysis had practically disappeared.

Two or three years after his healing, he was appointed Archbishop of Armagh and primate of Ireland. In that position he worked fearlessly for reconciliation in an ecumenical partnership with the Roman Catholic Cardinal Tomas O Fiaich such as had not been seen in Northern Ireland before. He retired in 1986.

His healing was for me—and for all those who knew him and respected his ministry—an authentic sign of the kingdom of God. It demonstrated that we as Christians are healed that we might become servants for the Lord's healing in our society.